CORVETTES
OF THE
ROYAL CANADIAN NAVY
1939-1945

Distributed by:
Airlife Publishing Ltd
101 Longden Road, Shrewsbury SY3 9EB, England

Ken Macpherson and Marc Milner

CORVETTES
OF THE
ROYAL CANADIAN NAVY
1939-1945

Foreword by Louis C. Audette, O.C., Q.C.   Corvette Plans by John McKay

Canadian Cataloguing in Publication Data

Macpherson, Ken
        Corvettes of the Royal Canadian Navy, 1939-1945

Includes index.
ISBN 0-920277-83-7 HC
ISBN 1-55125-052-7 PB

1.   Corvettes (Warships). 2. Canada. Royal
Canadian Navy - History - World War, 1939-1945.
3.   World War, 1939-1945 - Naval operations, Canadian.
I. Milner, Marc. II. Title.

V825.5.C3M22 2000   940.54'5971   C00-930179-8

Hardcover edition printed 1993.

Design Susan Nicholson

Vanwell Publishing Limited
1 Northrup Crescent, Box 2131
St. Catharines, Ontario L2R 7S2

Printed in Canada

On the cover: HMCS *Arrowhead* 1943
Canadian Forces Photo Unit

On the back cover: HMCS *Sackville*
Corvette Sackville Trust

CONTENTS

Foreword *by L. C. Audette, O.C., Q.C.*

For the historian or researcher of tomorrow, few books about the Canadian navy will stir more memories than this one. The corvette was the backbone of the Canadian navy; it was the largest class of ships ever to serve in the Canadian navy and also the largest class of ships ever built in Canadian shipyards.

The Second World War gave rise to an extraordinary expansion in the Canadian navy; of the many thousands of Reserve officers and men who served in the war, few did not owe their early sea time at least in part to a corvette. The ships were marvels of seaworthiness and of personal discomfort; it must be remembered that they were designed before those at the top really gave adequate consideration to the needs of those at the bottom of the ladder.

For sheer worthiness, few ships have ever been better designed. Assigned to fight the U-boat menace, they were barely adequate in speed, their surface armament just met the needs of the moment, their anti-submarine Asdic equipment was barely adequate and their living conditions made heroes of men destined to quite other roles in life.

Whatever their faults and qualities, these fine little ships were productive of an esprit de corps which may not have existed elsewhere. Because the crews were numerically smaller than in frigates, destroyers and bigger ships, they were more closely knit and better known to their officers.

Today there remains only *Sackville* in Halifax to remind the world of a great past. Nevertheless, throughout the land, many men now old will keep in mind the days they spent in corvettes in harsher times. To them, this book will constitute a treasury of memories, and they are men who should not be forgotten.

L. C. Audette, O.C., Q.C., B.A., L.Ph., LL.B., D.Sc.Mil. (hon.)

Louis C. Audette was commissioned Lieutenant, RCNVR, in September 1939, and went to sea in HMCS Saguenay early in 1940. After Saguenay was torpedoed that December, he was transferred to HMCS St. Francis. He was appointed CO of the corvette Amherst in September 1942, leaving her in July 1944 to assume command of the new frigate Coaticook. When Coaticook left for the west coast in June 1945, Audette briefly commanded HMCS St. Catharines before taking his discharge.

Rejoining the navy in 1947, he commanded HMCS Carleton, the Naval Reserve Division at Ottawa, until his retirement in 1948 as Commander RCN(R). He has since held prominent office in several organizations dedicated to the rehabilitation of disabled persons.

Introduction & Acknowledgements

No other warship is so intimately connected with Canada's naval heritage as the ubiquitous corvette of the Second World War. It was, after all, the largest class of vessels ever to serve in the Canadian navy: 123 in various types. It was also the largest class of ships ever constructed in Canadian shipyards: 121 built between 1940 and 1944. These distinctions alone qualify the corvette for special status. It is probably true to say as well—although it has never been determined—that more Canadians went to sea in corvettes than in any other class of ship.

Perhaps more important than mere quantity was the quality of service provided to the nation by its corvettes. Corvettes carried Canada's naval effort through the darkest days of the Second World War. Without them the Battle of the Atlantic, the single most important campaign of the war, might well have gone the other way. As Admiral Sir Dudley Pound, First Sea Lord of the Royal Navy observed, "The Canadian corvettes solved the problem of the Atlantic convoys." In doing so the corvettes carved out for Canada and its navy a major role in the North Atlantic campaign, the only theatre of war ever commanded by a Canadian, and including primary responsibility—by 1944—for the close escort of the main convoys upon which the war effort in Europe depended. No other Canadian service achieved so much during the war, and much of that accomplishment was due to the eighty corvettes of the first two building programs that gave the RCN a central role in the difficult years of 1941-1943.

It is also true that the corvette fleet reflected all the strengths and weaknesses of the Canada of its day. In 1939 Canada had the industrial strength and population to build and man simple auxiliary war vessels in considerable numbers. Rudimentary weapons were available from First World War reserves, or from surplus

American and British production. But the war which these ships and men were called upon to fight was a modern, highly sophisticated one. Canada lacked the high-technology industry needed to provide the latest weapons and sensors for modern war. For the most part, though, corvettes did their job just by being there, providing the escorts upon which the whole system of trade defence was built. In the process they laid the foundations of the modern Canadian navy. It is no accident that Canada's National Naval Memorial, HMCS *Sackville*, is herself the last survivor of the corvette fleet.

Despite the importance of the corvette to Canadian history, no reliable history of the class has ever been published. This is a modest attempt to fill that gap. What follows is a concise, popular account of the corvette in Canadian service during the Second World War: its design, equipment, employment, modifications, victories, losses and final disposal. Although it does not pretend to be the definitive history of the class, what follows is based on extensive research in documentary and secondary sources, and on the sharing of research by other scholars. Those interested in more reading about various aspects of the corvette story are referred to the following:

John McKay and John Harland's *Anatomy of the Ship: Flower Class Corvette AGASSIZ* (London, 1993) provides an extraordinarily detailed examination of the subject, and we gratefully acknowledge John McKay's permission to include some of his beautifully drawn plans in our book.

G. N. Tucker, *The Naval Service of Canada*, Vol. II, (Ottawa, 1952), the official history of RCN administration and shore activities, discusses the building programs, while Joseph Schull's *The Far Distant Ships* (Ottawa, 1950) provides an excellent parallel account of operations at sea; Peter Elliott, *Allied Escort Ships of World War II* (London, 1977), is the most complete compendium of war-built classes; Antony Preston and Alan Raven, *Ensign 3: Flower Class Corvettes* (London, 1973), is a popular booklet with colour drawings of camouflage schemes (which we could not duplicate here); and there is extensive information on corvettes in Ken Macpherson and John

Burgess, *Ships of Canada's Naval Forces 1910-1985*, (Toronto, 1985). M. Milner, *North Atlantic Run: The Royal Canadian Navy and the Battle for the Convoys, 1939-1943* (Toronto, 1985) discusses the operational limitations and tactical employment of Canadian corvettes.

We have not attempted either to write or to illustrate a social history of the corvette: this book is primarily about the ships, not those who manned them. However, several personal accounts by Canadians are particularly notable for their reflections on corvette life: William Pugsley, *Saints, Devils and Ordinary Seamen* (Toronto, 1945); Alan Easton, *50 North* (Toronto, 1966); James Lamb, *Corvette Navy* (Toronto, 1977); Tom Blakely, *Corvette Cobourg* (Cobourg, privately published, 1985); H. Lawrence, *A Bloody War* (Toronto, 1979); and Frank Curry, *War At Sea: A Canadian Seaman on the North Atlantic* (Toronto, 1990).

Much of the material used here has been gleaned from documents held by the National Archives of Canada and the Directorate of History (DHist), NDHQ, both in Ottawa. The NAC's Record Group 24 contains extensive holdings on the origins and policy behind corvette acquisition and use. DHist also holds files on the corvette fleet and, in particular, the Naval Staff and Board Minutes, wherein much of the policy on the ordering, equipping and modernization of the corvette fleet is recorded. The periodic state of equipment in the corvette fleet is available from *Particulars of Canadian War Vessels*, held by DHist. Others have been mining these sources and have graciously shared their findings. We are particularly grateful to Dr Roger Sarty, Senior Historian at DHist, for sharing material from the NAC files and for reading the manuscript, and to John Harland for sharing his research. Among the many others who must be thanked for assisting the research we include, Gary Craigs, Anne Martin, and David Zimmerman.

Maurice Smith and Earl Moorehead, of the Marine Museum of the Great Lakes at Kingston, Helen Deroia, of the National Archives of Canada, and Michael Whitby, DHist, assisted with the illustrations. Any errors or omissions remain entirely our own.

PART I: *THE CLASS*

CHAPTER I

The Origins Of The Requirement And The Class

Although popular interest in navies centres on big ships—battleships, aircraft carriers and the like—all navies require auxiliary craft to carry out the multitude of routine functions essential to the exercise of maritime power. In the age of sail the great ships of the line provided the basis of naval power, but the daily chores of patrolling, escorting shipping and policing waters of vital interest fell to smaller craft: sloops, frigates, fourth- or fifth-rate ships of the line, and picket boats. Apart from frigates and the smaller ships of the line, most of these ships were acquired in time of war from the merchant fleet or were hastily built to meet immediate wartime needs. The experience of naval war in the twentieth century proved no different. Battle fleets with their attendant, specially built ships still formed the basis of maritime power, but the myriad tasks to be performed at sea required that auxiliary craft from merchant fleets, or hastily constructed in civilian yards, be obtained in large numbers.

Indeed, in the twentieth century the need for auxiliary craft was probably greater than ever before. The range and complexity of modern weapons forced an enormous expansion of coast and port defences in particular, and these required the support of many auxiliary vessels. Major ports depended upon controlled defensive minefields, anti-submarine and anti-torpedo nets and booms, examination services for merchant vessels passing in and out, a minesweeping capability to keep channels clear of enemy mines, seaward patrols by armed vessels and eventually the laying and maintenance of remote sensing devices such as seabed sonars. These tasks were in addition to those performed by harbour craft and the specifically offensive tasks of small, purpose-built warships like motor torpedo boats that supplemented the defensive system. In the First World War this great variety of tasks for auxiliary war vessels was expanded to include considerable fixed barriers in the crucial choke-points of traffic, such as the English Channel and the Straits of Gibraltar. In these activities trawlers and drifters, basically steam-powered fishing craft, did the lion's share of the work while a few heavily armed destroyers or patrol boats provided support.

Inshore patrols, minesweeping, minelaying, maintenance of harbour defence sonars, booms, anti-submarine nets, as well as policing those systems, was all the stuff of auxiliary craft from 1914-1918. The Royal Canadian Navy's experience in the First World War was largely one of small auxiliary craft. The major east coast ports of Halifax and Sydney both required the development of defensive systems built largely around auxiliary warships. To this vital, but hardly glamourous, work was added another by 1917, that of protecting merchant convoys from submarines. Prior to 1914 all navies discounted the threat to merchant shipping posed by submarines because submarines could not provide for the safety of civilian crew, and to imperil the lives of non-combatants contravened international law. Early in the twentieth century the biggest danger to shipping seemed to come from surface raiders, and their dependence on coal-fired steam—which severely limited range and required secure ports in which to coal ship and carry out maintenance—made such ships an easy mark for the pre-eminent naval power.

In the first year of the First World War Allied patrols swept the seas of surface raiders, while merchant shipping carried on as usual or was routed through "sanitized" zones. By 1917 there were four such zones in the Atlantic approaches to Britain, patrolled by a fleet of some four thousand ships, most of them auxiliary craft.

Such a system worked well against coal-fired surface raiders. However, diesel-powered submarines had both the range and the reliability to operate at sea for extended periods, and their ability to submerge allowed them to pass easily through the Allied blockade and avoid detection by surface patrols. Early in 1917 the Germans, previously restrained by international law and concern about what neutrals like the United States might do, turned their U-boats loose. In an all-out bid to knock Britain from the war, German submariners were given free rein to sink on sight any ships found in British waters. Losses to merchant shipping soared in the spring of 1917, causing widespread concern in naval circles.

The solution to the problem was to organize ocean-going shipping into convoys and to divert many of the auxiliary craft from useless patrols to close escort of them. When assisted by aircraft, which sharply limited the surface manoeuvrability of submarines and directed warships onto them, the escorted convoy system brought the danger from submarines under control. In the western Atlantic the Canadians had some experience with submarines in the last eighteen months of the war, when a number of large U-cruisers operated off Nova Scotia. In response to that threat the East Coast Patrol, a force of over one hundred trawlers and drifters based at Halifax, was developed, and some Canadian auxiliary craft served as well at Gibraltar. The submarine had thrust an important new role onto the auxiliary fleet.

After the Allied victory of 1918, the enormous fleet of auxiliaries was soon paid off. Much of the work was, of course, of a wartime nature only, and with peace there was no need for the elaborate coast and port defences. These defences would be impossibly expensive to maintain, and in any event by their very nature the small, simply built auxiliary craft could be quickly built or obtained in an emergency. What remained less clear in the interwar years was whether or not there was a need for still larger numbers of small ships as part of a future convoy system. German U-boat attacks on Allied shipping in the First World War had clearly contravened international law, and that "piracy" had brought the US into the war against Germany, sealing her fate. In any event, the submarine threat at its worst had been neutralized by a combination of convoys and airpower. It only remained to find a means of precisely locating a submarine once it submerged. The perfection in the 1920s of an active, ship-borne sonar (known in British and Commonwealth circles as ASDIC until 1945, the modern term will be used here) system seemed to promise easy and reliable underwater location of submarines—something which had always been a problem in the First World War. Simple logic dictated that the submarine had been beaten strategically by convoys and aircraft in 1917-1918, and with ship-borne sonar could now be defeated tactically. Not surprisingly the First Sea Lord of the British Admiralty claimed in 1938 that the Royal Navy's anti-submarine countermeasures were 80 percent effective. Moreover, in the 1930s all the major world powers reaffirmed their commitment to the laws of war, including that which protected merchant seamen from indiscriminate submarine attack. An assessment by the RCN in the late 1930s of the threat from submarines concluded that if international law was complied with, the threat from submarines would be slight. If a potential enemy did resort to unrestricted attacks, it was felt that the combination of convoy, airpower and modern weapons would so punish the submarines that they would soon be forced to give up their attacks.

Such was the mood as the RCN planned its fleet expansion in the darkening hours prior to the outbreak of the Second World War. Two factors determined the approach the RCN took to its ship acquisition in the late 1930s. The first was its long-standing desire, like all other navies, to build or obtain the largest fleet of "proper" warships that money and circumstance would permit. Warships proper were complex ships to build and run, and the Canadian experience of the First World War, when the U-cruisers raided the Canadian coast, was that such ships could not be acquired easily in war. Ships built to naval standards—quality of steel, arrangements of bulkheads, damage control, duplication of essential systems, fire control for weapons and the like—had, therefore, to be acquired in peace. The nature of the maritime threat to Canada, deemed to be limited to raids by large surface ships (probably cruisers, merchant raiders or U-cruisers again, and perhaps a battleship), also dictated that the RCN acquire ships with considerable power. At the end of 1938 the Naval Staff concluded that a fleet of eighteen large Tribal Class destroyers (HMCS *Haida*, preserved in Toronto, is the last surviving example of this class) would provide a credible deterrent force along Canada's coast. Concern for auxiliary vessels was also not far from the navy's mind at the end of the 1930s. The RCN built up stocks of equipment to convert civilian vessels to anti-submarine, minesweeping and other auxiliary tasks, and pressed the government to fund the construction of prototype small vessels. Four coal-fired minesweepers, the Fundy Class, were actually built in Canada and commissioned in 1938. However, the RCN was interested in a larger, more general-purpose naval design as the basis of a big auxiliary fleet expansion program.

As tensions with Germany increased in the spring of 1939, the RCN continued to press the British for their plans for the auxiliary war vessels needed to bring the fleet up to strength in the event of war. The return of an investigative committee of the National Research Council from a visit to Britain in July 1939 actually produced the first hard evidence of British plans for a class of ships known as Whale-Catchers as their principal auxiliary vessel. Based on a commercial whale-catcher design, these vessels were very basic small ships with good seakeeping capabilities, simple machinery and few creature comforts. They differed from most First World War auxiliary craft in two ways: they were larger, more capable ships and they were oil fired.

With the coming of war in September 1939, the RCN filled its requirements for auxiliary warships largely by taking control of government and civilian vessels. Unfortunately, few of these were up to the tasks demanded. It was also discovered that Canadian shipyards were incapable of building ships to naval standards. Simply ordering the required warships from British yards proved impossible—as it had in 1917-1918—because the yards were already tied up with British contracts. Nor would the British government allow skilled tradesmen to abandon their own jobs in order to provide Canada with the needed expertise. The RCN soon obtained the basic plans, courtesy of the NRC, for whale-catchers, but the ships clearly did not fit their major plans for fleet expansion, nor were they the kind of small vessel the RCN had in mind. The Canadians wanted to build a version of the British Halcyon Class minesweeper, proper warships, built to naval standards, and suitable for long-term service.

About the time the first British-built corvette, HMS *Gladiolus*, came down the slips in January 1940, the Canadians suggested that a barter scheme be established, whereby Canada would build whale-catchers—something Canadian industry could handle—and trade these ships to Britain for Tribal Class destroyers. While the details of the scheme were being sorted out, the RCN and Canadian government placed orders in Canadian yards for what were then known as Patrol Vessels. In the end sixty-four were originally ordered to Canadian account. It was expected that about half of these would go to the RN in trade for Tribals, while the balance would be assigned to Canadian ports as part of their defensive systems, and to replace the auxiliary vessels commandeered at the outbreak of the war.

In the spring of 1940 discussion of the barter scheme collapsed, apparently on the inability to find an equitable rate of exchange. In the event, Canada was allowed to order several Tribals from British yards. Ten contracts for Patrol Vessels building in Canada were transferred to the British, leaving fifty-four on order for the RCN: the sixty-four corvettes of what became the 1939-1940 construction program.

By the time the government got around to placing all the orders, the shipyards in the Maritime provinces were fully engaged with repairing war- and storm-damaged shipping, and so only three corvettes were ever built east of Quebec: all of them the products of the Saint John Shipbuilding and Drydock Company in New Brunswick. The balance of the corvette programs—and indeed the balance of wartime shipbuilding except for four destroyers commenced in Halifax mid-war—was completed in yards along the

"In the beginning..." **Battleford's** keel, Collingwood, Ontario, 3 October 1940.

The frames of **The Pas** begin to rise at Collingwood, 27 March 1941. The cradles for the two Scotch Marine boilers are also in place.

Barrie, her framing well advanced, seen from the starboard bow, Collingwood, 16 July 1940. This shot also clearly illustrates the bulkheads separating the two boiler rooms and the engine room.

Galt from astern, Collingwood, 3 October 1940. Her main deck is nearly plated-in, and the boiler and engine spaces are clearly visible in the midship section. The framing forward is for the raised forecastle. Neither Galt's stern, nor that of the unidentified corvette in the foreground, have yet been cut for depth charge chutes and minesweeping fairleads.

upper St Lawrence River, on the Great Lakes or the British Columbia coast. In essence, any firm that could bend boiler plate or drive rivets bid on the contracts, and Canada soon developed a vast shipbuilding industry. While this was a major accomplishment in its own right, and well in keeping with the government's hope that Canadian participation in the war could be largely industrial, the concentration of effort away from the Atlantic coast sowed the seeds of future crisis. A corvette, once fully fitted out for service on the east coast, could not return to the Great Lakes because it could no longer clear the sills of the locks. The seasonal nature of Great Lakes and St Lawrence navigation contributed to the problem of using shipyards there. The British Columbia coast was, of course, thousands of miles and many weeks' steaming away from the corvettes' principal operational theatre in the Atlantic. By 1943 the inaccessibility of the industry which built the corvettes contributed to the crisis over their modernization.

The possibility that the corvettes might have to be extensively altered was not even on the horizon of RCN thinking in the summer of 1940. The problem then was how to tackle the very considerable expansion in fleet size the 1939-1940 corvette program promised. The first program alone required over three hundred new officers and the RCN lacked the facilities to house and train them. Despite the scale of the problem, the tremendous increase in the auxiliary fleet was not seen as the portent of great things in 1940. Clearly corvettes did not represent the RCN's interest, although they were seen as having good public relations value. Although the British dubbed them "Flower Class Corvettes" and gave them the names of flowers (it being thought a nice irony to boast publicly that a deadly U-boat had been destroyed by the likes of HMS *Buttercup*), the RCN took a different tack. After all, as Admiral Nelles, the Chief of the Naval Staff observed, flowers don't knit mittens. So the Canadian corvettes were named after Canadian communities, and local support for the ships was actively sought. Sponsors, often the wife of the mayor or some other local dignitary of the town from which the corvette took its name, were provided at launchings by local communities. Dishes and silverware for the wardroom, and personal comforts such as magazines and woollen clothing were provided by municipalities and local service clubs. And where possible, the newly commissioned corvettes—or at

least their new captains—paid a courtesy call on the town itself. It was a superb idea.

For a brief period then, Canadian corvettes were known as Town Class Corvettes, a classification soon abandoned when the British applied the class name of Town to the fifty First World War-vintage destroyers acquired from the US in 1940. Canadian corvettes therefore lost their distinctive classification, although the practice of naming them for towns continued—with some exceptions, as will be noted. It says a great deal about the navy's modest plans for these ships that most of the names chosen for the first construction program were from rather small communities. The three ships building in Saint John, for example, were named for towns on the Nova Scotia-New Brunswick border: *Amherst*, *Moncton*, and *Sackville*. Some communities, such as Bathurst, New Brunswick, and Churchill, Manitoba, were on the original name list for the first program as well, but were dropped because of conflicts in the shared British Commonwealth ship-name lists. Bathurst became *Buctouche*, another small New Brunswick town, while Churchill was changed to *Moose Jaw*. Others such as Banff and Jasper, which became *Wetaskiwin* and *Kamloops* respectively, had actually been launched before the names changed.

It was unfortunate that the RCN's attempt to distinguish its corvettes from British ones lapsed. Despite their outward similarities, such as the main armament of a 4-inch breech-loading main gun and depth charges (discussed in the next chapter) the two navies developed quite different ships. While British corvettes were quickly drawn into anti-submarine warfare and ocean escort of convoys, the Canadian ships of the first construction program were developed for genuine auxiliary roles. For example, to overcome the shortage of minesweepers, all of the first program were reconfigured as auxiliary minesweepers. This entailed moving the galley from its quarterdeck location in British plans to just forward of the boiler room, leaving additional space on the quarterdeck for the steam winch. The shape of the stern itself was changed from its original fine lines to a broader, squarer shape to accommodate both the fairleads for the sweep gear and the depth charge rails. When it was noted that this extra weight tended to raise the bow slightly and might possibly affect the ship's sonar, the trade-off was considered acceptable. In any event, the original corvette design tended to trim by the bow and the

*One of **The Pas'** fire-tube boilers under construction at Collingwood, 1 August 1941, its size well illustrated by the riveter in the right-hand firebox.*

***Galt's** boilers and engines going aboard, Collingwood, 23 December 1940.*

Collingwood, *immediately after her launching on 27 July 1940 from Collingwood Shipyards, displays very well the lines of the hull and deck houses in the original design.*

Few photos illustrate the small size of corvettes as well as this one of **Buctouche** *at Lauzon, Quebec, two months prior to commissioning in June 1941. This shot also shows the inadequacy of the bridge in the original design. The tiny compass house on top of the superstructure held the sonar set, and the small deck surrounding it had to accommodate secondary armament, signalling equipment, the bridge lookouts, the officer of the watch and, at action stations, the captain as well.*

Canadian alterations may have inadvertently compensated for the design flaw.

The other visible Canadian change was the position of the after gun tub. In the original British design the mainmast was located well aft on the engine room casing, in order to give a proper spread for the aerial. The after gun position was then placed between the mainmast and the funnel, making it impossible to fire the gun directly aft and risking damage to the mast itself. The RN quickly modified this by the removal of the mainmast, since a free arc of fire for the main anti-aircraft gun was deemed of paramount importance. Since the RCN's corvettes were expected to operate in the Western Atlantic, A/A defence was not a priority. The Canadian solution was to reverse the position of the mainmast and the gun tub, placing the gun position well aft—a distinctive feature of all subsequent Canadian corvettes. The mainmast was discarded after the first few corvettes were completed, but the gun position remained as a major identifying feature of Canadian corvettes. Despite the decision to eliminate the mainmast, the foremast remained ahead of the bridge in all designs until 1943. The foremast carried a crows-nest, an essential feature of pre-radar ships, and its original position facilitated voice communication with the bridge.

There were other, much less noticeable, differences between the corvettes of the first Canadian construction program and their British counterparts. Perhaps the most obvious was the secondary armament. While the British quickly allotted a 2-pdr pom-pom to the after position and .50-calibre machine guns to the bridge wings, the Canadians lacked the necessary guns. As a result, most Canadian corvettes carried only .50-calibre machine guns in the after position, often in two twin mountings. With the heavier machine guns aft, Canadian corvettes then settled for twin Lewis .303 machine guns on each of the bridge wings. The Lewis guns were just about all the original bridge design could handle, and, while they gave a few members of the crew something to do, they were of little value in battle with a U-boat. Canadian-pattern wireless sets and Canadian refrigeration were other local modifications, both of which proved successful.

Far and away the most important—and least noticeable—of the differences between British and Canadian corvettes at the outset was in the provision of gyro compasses. These electronically controlled and stabilized compasses were connected to repeaters mounted as required throughout the ship—the wheelhouse, sonar hut, radar room, bridge, etc. Each gyro compass repeater was graduated in 360 degrees and indicated the ship's heading and magnetic north. No matter how much the ship pitched or yawed, the indicators on the face of the repeater (commonly known as a pelorus, which was actually the metal ring with sighting pieces mounted on gimbals on the outer edge of the compass) gave steady and true readings. Canada had only a limited supply of gyro compasses, and it was decided to fit them to its small fleet of Bangor Class minesweepers, the ships designed and built as the RCN's principal minesweeping vessels. Their intended function made their requirement for accurate navigation clearly greater, but the decision to fit Bangors with gyros was also occasioned by the need to provide the 'sweepers with a retractable-dome sonar (which would not get fouled in the sweep wires). By 1939 all such sonars required gyro compasses and so the Bangors got the best compasses—and the best sonars.

In contrast, the corvettes were fitted with simple magnetic compasses, mounted on a single binnacle inside the compass shelter (also known as the Asdic hut or charthouse) on the bridge. Its needle was not stabilized and the compass face was graduated in thirty-two "points." The difference between the two

compasses not only influenced the handling of individual ships and the accuracy of depth charge attacks, but also made it extremely difficult to coordinate the activities of ships working in company. For example, the bearings on a gyro compass between north and east are graded from 0 to 90 degrees. Magnetic compasses divided that section into eight points: north-by-east, north-northeast, northeast-by-north, northeast, northeast-by-east, east-northeast, east-by-north and east.

Magnetic compasses were suitable for rudimentary navigation and whale-catching, but they were not up to the standards of modern war. The needle swayed with every movement of the ship, so that headings and true north had to be inferred from a guesstimate of the needle's mean position. The compass was also subject to error induced by the shock of firing depth charges or the main gun. After one action, the captain of Amherst sailed under darkness and cloud for a day before discovering that the shock of gunfire, pounding of explosives and heavy seas had reset his compass by 135 degrees. Nor were there any repeaters: the ship's single compass was inside the charthouse. It was impossible, for example, for the corvette's captain to be on the open bridge during a convoy battle and watching the magnetic compass inside at the same time. With a simpler compass came a very basic sonar, the Type 123A, reserved in the RN for trawlers and below since the early 1930s. The decision to fit the corvettes with magnetic compasses allowed them to be completed without the low-power electrical system associated with the gyro compass-fitted ships. Initially, the absence of an LP system was not a problem, but later it meant that significant modernization could not be carried out until the ships had such a system installed.

In late 1940 the Canadians also learned that the RN was modifying its original corvette design to lengthen the forecastle in order to improve seakeeping and crew accommodation. The RCN was well aware of these structural changes, but saw no reason to delay completion of the first program, probably because the original design was adequate to the task envisaged for Canada's burgeoning corvette fleet.

In most other respects the 1939-1940 corvette program conformed to the original British design. The ships had an overall length of 205', breadth of 33' 1", drew a maximum of 15.5' of water aft and displaced about 950 tons. The propulsion system was a simple and long familiar merchant marine plant, which suited both operation and maintenance under conditions of wartime expansion. The 4-cylinder triple-expansion engines produced 2750 horsepower and a maximum of 185 rpm. This was an open type engine, with its moving parts and lubrication points easily accessible to the engineers. The two boilers fitted in each ship of the first construction program were equally simple Scotch Marine "fire-tube" type. These held the water inside the huge drum of the boiler and the "fire" was shot through it in tubes which started in the three fireboxes at the bottom and then snaked back and forth through the drum. These were the simplest and cheapest of boilers to make. However, they apparently were chosen because the large volume of water contained in the boiler held a considerable reserve of steam for quick acceleration: just what was needed in the final thrust for a whale—or a submarine. The need to heat and contain such a large volume of water produced its own problems. The Scotch Marine boilers were slow at raising steam, and operated at comparatively low pressures (approximately 225 psi). They were also quite large, and so the original corvettes were limited to about 230 tons of fuel oil in the side bunkers abreast the boiler room. At a steady 12 knots a corvette had a range of 3500 nautical miles—about 1000 less at full speed of 16 knots. Some corvettes managed more speed and range, while age, shoddy wartime maintenance and construction and hull condition conspired to deliver less in many ships.

Early reports indicated that the ships performed well. As the Admiralty informed Ottawa in early 1941, corvettes demonstrated "seamanlike handling" and could withstand "without material damage the heaviest gale in the North Atlantic." Heavy seas did slow them down appreciably, however. Maximum speed could only be maintained up to a "sea state" of two. In a sea state four, speed was reduced to eleven knots, with a 50 percent reduction in sonar efficiency, and in a sea state six the ships had to reduce to six knots and their sonars became ineffective. In heavier seas corvettes had either to run with the sea on their quarter or heave-to and ride it out. Steerage was difficult at anything less than 3 knots in ideal conditions. Based as it was on a whale-catcher design, the corvette was an agile ship, with a corklike response to the sea and very responsive handling. It was designed to turn a complete circle in one hundred seconds and could easily out-manoeuvre a surfaced or submerged U-boat.

The corvette, in its original design, was a very simple ship intended for very simple tasks of comparatively short duration. Perhaps nowhere is this more evident than in early plans for crew size and accommodation. The original complement was twenty-nine all ranks, but the earliest evidence of crew size for Canadian corvettes suggested a total of four officers and forty-eight ratings, as follows:

1 Lieutenant Commander, as Captain
1 Lieutenant, RCN(R)
2 Lieutenants, or Sub Lieutenants, RCN(VR)
1 Chief Petty Officer
3 Leading Seamen
12 Able or Ordinary Seamen
1 Leading Telegraphist
1 Telegraphist
1 Telegraphist Signalman
1 Signalman
1 Engineer Officer, or Chief Engine Room Artificer
3 ERAs
3 Stoker POs
6 Leading Stokers
10 Stokers
1 UPO or LVA
2 Cooks
2 Stewards

Among these crewmen were the following weapons and sensor specialists (non-substantive ratings):

1 Telegraphist Coder
1 Leading Coder
2 Quarters Ratings (Gunnery Specialists)
1 Leading Torpedoman (in charge of Depth Charges and Electronics)
2 Seamen Torpedomen
3 High Signals Detection Ratings (Sonar operators)
3 Signals Detection Operators

As the size of the crew and the complexity of the weapons and sensors increased, the number of specialists and support personnel grew as well. By 1941 radar, anti-aircraft and more signal ratings had been added, as had an additional officer.

Accommodation in corvettes was in three main areas; forward of the deckhouse in the area immediately below the 4-inch gun, within and immediately below the deckhouse, and aft of the engine room. The latter was originally divided into officers' cabins, probably in keeping with the naval tradition that officers were accommodated aft (HMCS *Haida*, a wartime Tribal class destroyer preserved in Toronto, has berthing for officers aft). Later plans show the space aft developed for Chiefs and POs, and in some ships the engineering staff took over the after mess. Officers came to find their place within the deckhouse, which gave them quick and easy access to the bridge. The captain's cabin and officers' wardroom, toilet and sleeping accommodation were below the wheelhouse. In time, the fifth officer to join the ship typically found himself sleeping on the wardroom settee. Crew accommodation was forward, originally divided into separate sleeping and messing spaces. Initially, the lower level was reserved for Chiefs and POs. Seamen were accommodated on the main deck level, with direct access to the weather deck through a lobby in the open well of the forecastle. Gradually both the main and lower deck messes were turned over to seamen, who, crowded into spaces designed for less than half their number, ate, slept and relaxed wherever they could in the forward messes.

Little is known of the development of RCN plans for the corvettes as they lay building in yards all over the country through 1940 and early 1941. The collapse of Norway, the Low Countries and France in the spring and early summer of 1940 radically changed the nature of the war. All the RCN's available strength—essentially its six pre-war River Class destroyers—went overseas in response to the crisis and soon found themselves based in Scotland doing convoy escort duty. But this change does not appear to have affected the RCN's plans for its corvettes. The focus of naval expansion was still on Tribal Class destroyers, which would have a long-term value to a postwar fleet. The RCN did acquire more destroyers in the fall of 1940, in the form of six ex-USN Towns: aged, First World War four-stacker destroyers which the RCN took over reluctantly from the British. This unexpected increase foreshadowed the major expansion of the fleet scheduled for 1941, when the bulk of the first construction program corvettes were due to arrive. However, it was the corvettes, in the end, that formed what Nelles called "the stepping stones of fleet expansion." Finding the men to crew the large number of auxiliary ships on the way for 1941 was a daunting task, particularly since the facilities to house and train them had not yet been built.

If plans to develop training facilities for the men who would man the corvette fleet lacked urgency in late 1940, it was probably because well into 1941 it was

still intended to use the corvettes themselves as jacks-of-all-trades in conjunction with the system of defended ports along the coast. Corvettes would be needed to replace unsuitable civilian and government ships commandeered for a variety of tasks in 1939, and the surplus from those requirements were to be assigned to the ports to form anti-submarine hunting groups of two ships, or double groups of five (allowing for one spare). These groups were to undertake patrols of only several days in the approaches to harbours, presumably searching for submarines or checking out contacts. It seemed likely as well that the corvettes would form part of the local anti-submarine escort which shepherded convoys through the submarine danger zone in the approaches to assembly ports. Corvettes in excess of Canadian home needs were to be sent overseas to serve alongside the RN at the discretion of the British.

The crisis of the summer of 1940 led the RCN to place further orders for corvettes—sixteen in all—of what became the 1940-1941 building program. Six of these ships, *Brantford*, *Dundas*, *Midland*, *New Westminster*, *Timmins*, and *Vancouver*, were repeats of the first fifty-four Canadian corvettes without the auxiliary minesweeping gear. Their resemblance to the original fifty-four—notably the position of the after gun tub—but without the distinctive minesweeping davits astern, sets them apart. The rest of the 1940-1941 program brought major changes to hull configuration as a result of wartime experience and produced a separate type within the class: these ships will be discussed in the next chapter.

The 1940-1941 program also introduced new, water-tube, boilers. The Scotch Marine boilers were not a success. They delivered the rapid burst of speed as planned, but the increased speed could not be sustained. Moreover, a steady maximum—or near-maximum—speed caused failures in the boilers themselves. The water-tube type offered a somewhat less responsive but more reliable supply of steam. In this type the main body of the boiler acted as a firebox and water passed through it in banks of tubes. Such boilers were smaller, lighter, easier to maintain, operated at slightly higher pressures and were considered safer. From a cold start they could raise steam faster, but they did lack that reserve of steam needed for a quick increase in speed. However, once the boiler output was raised to its higher limits it could sustain the pressures without fear of damage. In later

Morden on builder's trials, August 1941. With the exception of the greatly extended bridge wings, she is a fine example of the original Canadian design.

New Westminster shortly after commissioning at Victoria in early 1942. She, and four other sisters in the 1940-1941 program, were the last of the short-forecastle corvettes and the first to fit water-tube boilers. What distinguishes them from the first building program is the absence of minesweeping davits on the quarterdeck.

designs the smaller, lighter water-tube boilers would be exploited by using the space and weight saved to increase oil capacity. For the moment, however, the 1940-1941 program simply made the switch in types, with no appreciable improvement in performance of the ships, save perhaps reliability.

By the end of 1940, four corvettes of the 1939-1940 RCN construction program were in commission, with fifty still to complete, and sixteen on order as part of the 1940-1941 program: a total of seventy corvettes on order to Canadian account. The ten corvettes building in Canadian yards to British account were given priority and were the first to sail at the end of 1940. These ships differed significantly from their Canadian contemporaries. They were built to the original British design, without minesweeping gear, with a fine duck-tail stern, galley aft of the engine room and the after gun position well forward.

The first two Canadian-built British corvettes, *Trillium* and *Windflower*, departed Halifax for Britain in the first week of December. All Canadian-built RN corvettes were in British waters by March 1941. The RCN manned them for passage only with skeleton crews and, in most cases, only small-arms—rifles and Lewis guns—for armament. *Hepatica* was equipped for passage with a dummy wooden 4-inch main gun which arrived badly warped, causing one RN ship to ask by signal lamp if the RCN was "beating the enemy to death." Once in the UK it proved difficult for the RCN to get the Admiralty to take over the ships, perhaps because they too lacked a gyro compass. In fact, the British soon put these undermanned and ill-prepared Canadian corvettes to work with the Clyde Escort Force, alongside the Canadian destroyers, escorting convoys. In the end, Canadian inability to obtain release of their crews led the Admiralty to agree to their commissioning into the RCN: the only Canadian corvettes to carry flower names. Significantly, these ships remained British property, and the Admiralty took care of their maintenance and refits. For this reason, they were the first corvettes in Canadian service to receive the latest equipment and to be modernized.

The 1939-1940 corvette building program was one of the most remarkable feats of Canadian ship construction ever. In a little less than two years seventy ships went from the planning stages into service. By the

The control equipment for the Type 123A sonar. The magnetic compass binnacle on the right carries the handwheel used to rotate the sonar dome under the ship, while its bearing was read off the compass. The recorder on the left produced a "trace" of the sonar signal while the operator listened on headphones.

end of 1941 all but one of the original program—at a cost of about $600,000 per ship—were in service. But building simple hulls and basic machinery to standards which were, by 1939, long familiar even to Canadian industry, proved to be the easy part. Even as the products of the first construction program poured down the St Lawrence River behind the spring freshet of 1941, the war they were entering was entirely different from that envisaged at their conception. It would tax to their limits both the ships and the men destined to serve in them.

Windflower *at Halifax in December 1940, shortly before leaving for Britain. As one of the ten corvettes built for the RN in the first program, she carries her after gun position forward of the engine room skylight. The engine room casing is extended well aft to accommodate the galley, and she has no minesweeping gear fitted. She also has no armament other than depth charges—and only one thrower per side.*

CHAPTER II

The First Construction Program Goes To War 1941

The expansion of the Canadian corvette fleet in early 1941 was delayed by the influences of season and distance. Only *Cobalt*, *Chambly*, and *Collingwood*, commissioned on the east coast by the end of 1940, and only one of the BC-built ships, *Wetaskiwin*, had entered service. The next three, *Agassiz* in January 1941, *Alberni* in February and *Kamloops* in March, also commissioned from west coast yards. With the coming of spring, however, the pace intensified. The first east coast corvettes of 1941 reached Halifax in late April: *Orillia*, *Pictou*, and *Rimouski*. In May ten more were added to the list and the ten British Flowers sent to the UK with Canadian crews were transferred to the RCN. In all, between December 1940 and May 1941 thirty-three corvettes—more than half of the 1939-1940 construction program (British orders included)—were added to the Canadian navy. Most of the rest followed before the end of the year. The last to complete from the first batch, *Moncton*, was delayed by urgent demands on the resources of Maritime yards for repair work, and did not commission until April 1942. On average, the ships had taken ten months to complete, slightly longer than their British counterparts.

Although conceived as journeyman auxiliary vessels, the world into which the first Canadian corvettes were born soon thrust a new role upon them. The British found that their prewar preparations for anti-submarine warfare were no match for the resourcefulness of the Germans. The RN considered the submarine an inshore threat prior to the Second World War, largely because the combination of airpower and convoy had made it difficult for the Germans to find and attack shipping on the open seas. It was assumed that to find targets submariners had to operate well inshore, in the approaches to harbours and focal points of shipping: to survive in these heavily patrolled waters they would have to operate submerged.

German submariners had different ideas. They preferred more freedom of movement—on the surface—and kept well out to sea where, in the first year of the war, they found plenty of unescorted and unconvoyed shipping. The British responded by convoying more ships and extending the range of air patrols and anti-submarine escorts. The latter included their fleet of corvettes, which now found themselves cast in the role of ocean escorts for merchant convoys. The Germans in turn simply moved farther to seaward. In the summer of 1940 they also began to attack convoys using roving groups of U-boats known as Wolf Packs. These packs located convoys by combing the sea lanes, coordinating their movements through direct and continuous high frequency (HF) radio communications with shore-based plotting staffs, who in turn ordered changes in deployment according to the latest intelligence on Allied shipping. When a convoy was located, the pack was brought together in its vicinity. The attack normally took place at night, with the U-boats running in through the escorting screen on the surface like motor torpedo boats. Once through the convoy the U-boats either ran away at high speed or simply submerged into the tangle of wakes behind the merchant ships.

Such wolf pack attacks proved devastating during the winter of 1940/41—what German submariners called the Happy Time. The RN lacked the means to deal effectively with them, other than to extend the range of anti-submarine escort farther into the Atlantic. As they did so the Germans again moved farther out to sea. By April 1941 the RN was providing anti-submarine escort of convoys as far west as Iceland, and in that month extended the range of their destroyer and corvette escort groups beyond Iceland by developing bases there. With these facilities, and by employing corvettes for ocean escort duty, the British could protect convoys to about 35 degrees west.

The corvettes had to be substantially modified for the new mid-ocean anti-submarine escort role. There were now four depth charge throwers fitted amidships instead of the original two, more depth charges, heavier secondary armament of 20-mm guns carried on extended and strengthened bridge wings, radar and more signalling equipment. All of these added to the size of the crew, which required more accommodation. The original corvette crew size swelled from under fifty to eighty within a year and eventually to nearly one hundred. Men slept and ate where they could until the ships were modified.

Further, the change from short voyages in the short seas of coastal waters gave way to very long voyages amid the towering swells of the deep ocean. The early design was safe enough, but the bluff bows of the tiny ships often cut into oncoming waves before they could rise completely out of the trough. Solid walls of seawater then swept the forecastle, cascaded into the open well deck and soaking all inside. Overcrowding added to the misery. British designers attempted to overcome both problems by redesigning the forward portion of the corvette. The forecastle deck was extended aft, nearly to the funnel, a simple improvement which completely enclosed the open well deck and forward portion of the main deck. The extended forecastle provided increased accommodation, and improved habitability (and in the Canadian design would permit access to the galley without the need to venture outside).

It was possible to add these features to the corvettes already in service, and these improvements and others were incorporated into the design of later corvettes. For example, new bows, noticeably higher, with increased flare to keep them from plunging, were designed. The bridge was also raised in the process to make the wheelhouse level with the forecastle deck. In this interim stage the bridge retained the original mercantile design, but a second magnetic compass binnacle was added forward of the compass shelter. The foremast, for the moment, remained ahead of the bridge. Further modifications included the introduction of water-tube boilers in separate compartments, for reasons of safety and efficiency, although with no increase in horsepower or speed. The modifications pushed displacement up to 1,015 tons, increased draught aft to 15'7" and lengthened the ship to 208'.

Ten of these ships, which the RCN knew as Revised Patrol Vessels—or RPVs—were ordered as part of the 1940-1941 building program. Like other batches of corvettes, the RPVs were distinctive in appearance. Their fine lines forward nicely complemented the gentle rise in the stern of the original design, giving the ships a noticeable sweep from stem to stern. The new bow with extended forecastle, topped by a bridge of original mercantile design, set them apart from the earlier ships and the Modified Classes which followed.

While the RN introduced these major changes to its new construction, it also began a modernization of the earlier ships, extending the forecastle and improving their weapons, electronics, accommodation and habitability. All of this was intended to change the corvette from a very rudimentary auxiliary vessel, to a front-line combatant in the major operational campaign of the Atlantic war. The British corvette fleet was therefore undergoing significant change even as the first Canadian corvettes went into service off Nova Scotia.

In the winter of 1940/41 the RCN's few corvettes conducted patrols from Halifax and Sydney, and shared some of the burden of local anti-submarine escort of

Corvettes alongside at Halifax, 1941. The splinter mats and extended bridge wings and absence of a mainmast mark the corvette farthest left as British-owned. The three inboard ships are all from the first RCN building program, all still with unextended bridge wings and mainmasts aft of the funnel. One also carries a Canadian-designed and -built SW1C radar at the masthead.

Collingwood *(inboard),* **Cobalt** *and* **Chambly***, Halifax, 6 May 1941. The minesweeping gear fitted to the first RCN program ships shows clearly on the quarterdeck; no secondary armament has yet been fitted and* **Collingwood** *shows only one starboard thrower. The antenna atop* **Chambly's** *foremast was fitted for sea trials of what became the SW1C radar.*

convoys to the limits of Canadian responsibility—typically some four hundred miles to seaward. At that point an ocean escort of battleships, cruisers or even submarines took charge of the convoy to protect it from the anticipated mid-Atlantic threat of German surface raiders. This pattern, begun in September 1939, remained unchanged until the spring of 1941, when it became clear that the major threat even in the mid-ocean was from submarines. The extension of British anti-submarine escort to 35 degrees west left one major gap in anti-submarine protection of convoys between Iceland- and Nova Scotia-based escorts. In May 1941, therefore, the British Admiralty asked Canada to establish a base at St John's, Newfoundland, and use its burgeoning fleet of corvettes to fill that gap. Canada complied and the Newfoundland Escort Force (NEF) was born.

With the establishment of the NEF, the RCN made a substantial change in the employment of the corvette fleet. Instead of using them to augment the patrols of the defended ports, in limited hunting roles, or simply sending those in excess of Canadian requirements to serve overseas at British discretion, the RCN's corvettes were committed to the defence of a convoy system onto which the U-boats were already drawn. The ships, designed and intended as a reaction and hunting force—really part of a general deterrence within a geographical area—would now have to defend vulnerable targets from an aggressive and skilled enemy. They would have to do so in one of the most difficult theatres of war, noted for the ferocity of its gales, its numbing cold and heavy seas. Moreover, St John's was to be a Canadian base and the maintenance of NEF a Canadian responsibility. Unfortunately, there was little in St John's or the RCN itself to support either the ships or the men in a major operation of war. While the corvettes themselves could easily survive the rigours of oceanic service, it was not clear that the men could, or that they could develop and maintain a high level of fighting effectiveness in the process.

Although armed with rudimentary anti-submarine weaponry, Canada's corvettes posed little threat to a skilled submariner in 1941. Their principal anti-submarine weapons were an antiquated sonar, about sixty depth charges and a 1914-vintage 4-inch gun. Like most Second World War sonars, the Type 123A carried by RCN corvettes projected a sound beam from a fixed transducer mounted under the hull. The transducer could be rotated by a handwheel through

*The main secondary armament of Canadian corvettes until 1943, twin .50-calibre machine guns, in this case on the bridge wing of **Shediac**.*

360 degrees, but the sound beam was fixed at an angle of about 6 degrees below horizontal, with about a 10-degree cone. Range and depth of a submerged target were determined by simple mathematics. The time interval between transmission of a signal and the return echo gave the range, and once that was estimated, depth was a matter of geometry. The sonar had a maximum range of 2500 yards under ideal conditions, but was dependent on good conditions and a skilled operator to get useful results. And because the transducer was fixed in the horizontal plane, the ability to maintain contact with a target was a function of the target's depth and range. Unless the submarine was very close to the surface, contact was lost at ranges less than a few hundred yards. Conversely, if the submarine was very deep, and sonar conditions poor, the ship might have to stand off so far that no contact could be made. Good Asdic ratings (sonarmen) were crucial to the success of the equipment, and personnel selection officers screened potential candidates for their ability to discriminate pitch and tone. Musicians were considered particularly good raw material.

The imprecision of the sonar was matched by that of the corvette's main anti-submarine weapon, depth charges. The purpose of these weapons was not to blow up the submarine in the way of conventional munitions, but rather to work in conjunction with the water to crush the sub's pressure hull. Each depth charge weighed approximately 420 pounds, of which some 300 was explosive (initially TNT, later "Torpex" or "Minol"). They were detonated by a hydrostatic (water

*Instruction in the corvette's main gun: **Arvida's** 4-inch Mk.IX BL gun. Ready-use shells for the gun's two-part ammunition can just be seen in brackets around the edge of the gun platform. The illumination rocket rails on the gunshield were fitted sometime after 1942.*

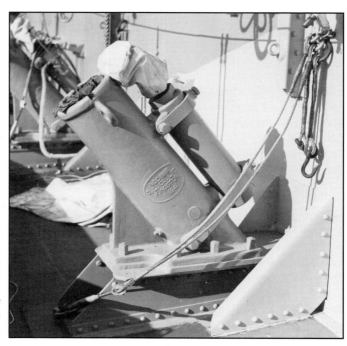

*All RCN corvettes were fitted with the Mk.II depth charge thrower, seen here aboard **Owen Sound** in November 1943. The thrower was actually a mortar. The firing charge was placed at the top of the small tube (under the canvas cover), which carried the explosion to the base of the ejector.*

pressure-sensitive) pistol that could be set to detonate at depths from 50 to 350 feet throughout most of the war, and later down to 600 feet. Half of the charges, typically those in one of the two rails at the stern and beside one of each of the two throwers per side were "heavy," carrying additional weights to help them sink faster. By the middle of the Second World War these depth charges were normally delivered on a submerged target in patterns of ten. The idea was to catch the submarine inside a three-dimensional, double-diamond -shaped explosion and crush it. Once the setting was given and the order to fire received, two charges were dropped astern first, then two charges thrown from the sides, then two more stern-dropped charges, followed by the next two fired from the throwers and finally two last charges from the stern rails.

It all sounds easy enough, but depth charge attacks took considerable skill and a large measure of luck to be accurate. The corvette had to establish position, course, speed and depth of the target ahead, plot a course to intercept it and then at a given point race ahead—losing sonar contact—and drop the charges into the submarine's anticipated position. The run-in left the ship effectively blind and gave submariners, who could hear the corvette's changes in speed and direction, time to take evasive action.

If the submarine was blown to the surface—as was often the case—the corvette had two options. The 4-inch Mk.IX gun fired a 31-pound projectile about 12,000 yards. Corvettes normally carried 220 rounds, a third of which until late 1943 were starshell illumination rounds. At anything beyond point-blank range it was hard to hit reliably with the 4-inch from a rolling and yawing corvette. Not infrequently the main gun was used simply to drive the U-boat down before its superior surface speed (18 knots) carried it out of range entirely.

Perhaps not surprisingly then, the method of sinking surfaced U-boats frequently used by corvette captains was ramming. Although a U-boat was faster, the corvette could outmanoeuvre a surfaced submarine. Moreover, unlike destroyers, which often attempted to ram at such a speed that their bows were out of the water, corvettes were slow enough to ensure that their gently curving bow struck the submarine's pressure hull squarely before riding over. Such attacks did considerable damage to the corvette—and one senior British naval engineer opined in 1942 that with all the latest weapons, escorts were still content to

bludgeon the enemy to death—but the trade-off for a U-boat kill was well worth it.

It seems fair to say that these early corvettes were not much of a threat to a skilled submariner. Indeed, the officer in charge of the training of Canadian corvettes assigned to Newfoundland in the summer of 1941 was appalled at the inaccuracy of ships' gunnery. He observed rather caustically, after one training exercise in September, that, "At present most corvettes are equipped with one weapon of approximate precision—the ram!" However, *destroying* submarines was not what NEF was all about. Those inshore jacks-of-all-trades—and clearly masters of none—made their way to St John's in late May and June of 1941 to begin the escort and protection of mercantile convoys across the vile North Atlantic, a task for which they will always be remembered.

The first ships to arrive as part of NEF were a small group of corvettes from Halifax composed of *Agassiz*, *Alberni*, *Chambly*, *Cobalt*, *Collingwood*, *Orillia*, and *Wetaskiwin*. These constituted the total disposable strength of corvettes on the east coast (the others were still fitting out or working up). Five of the ships were commanded by reservists from the merchant marine (RCNR) and two—*Chambly*, and *Wetaskiwin*—by professional naval officers (RCN). In this sense the group was not typical of the corvette fleet which, on the whole, became the preserve of Volunteer Reservists, the RCNVR, young men with little or no previous experience at sea enlisted for the war only. The officer in charge of this small initial deployment was Commander James Douglas "Chummy" Prentice, RN (retired), a Victoria, BC, native who had joined the RN before the First World War and retired to BC in the 1930s. Prentice was a genuine character, noted for his cigar and monocle and his driving ambition to whip the escort fleet into shape. He thought well of corvettes as anti-submarine ships and would be rewarded for his efforts with what was long thought to be the first known Canadian U-boat kill.

To build the NEF to its required strength the RCN's destroyers were assigned, including those operating in British waters, as were the ten RCN Flowers also based in Britain in the spring of 1941. New corvettes, as they commissioned, were sailed to St John's during the rest of 1941. By the end of that year fully 75 percent of the RCN ocean-going escort strength was committed to the NEF, including nearly sixty corvettes.

The Mk.II depth charge thrower fired off the carrier, or stock, as well as the depth charge itself. The carriers, seen here being manhandled by **Morden's** port thrower crews, had to be loaded first.

The corvette's principal weapon was the depth charge: a 420-pound drum of high explosive and steel projected from throwers or rolled off rails astern. Once the carrier was inserted into the thrower, the charge was put in place: not an easy task on a heaving ship and a wet deck. Here **Mayflower's** crew tackles the job of loading a "heavy" charge (note the weight on the end).

Virtually without exception, the ships and their crews were unprepared for the challenge of convoy escort in the North Atlantic. Although seaworthy enough to handle the weather, the corvettes had a violent motion in rough seas and it was said that they would roll on grass in a heavy dew. Too short to straddle the wave interval in the North Atlantic, corvettes climbed their way over—or smashed their way through—oncoming seas. They rose and fell like a runaway elevator as the ship passed through each crest and trough: messdecks, the quarterdeck, the bridge and the crew rising and falling thirty to fifty feet at a time. To the vertical motion was added the yawing and rolling of the ship, as they corkscrewed their way forward. Sailors young and old had to find their sea legs in a hurry, and many never could adjust to the motion. Some had to be sent to less arduous duty; others survived on liquid diets for days on end, watched knowingly by officers and crew to ensure that their health and their duties did not suffer unduly. Some, it must be said, enjoyed the sheer exhilaration of life at sea in a small ship.

Water dominated a corvette sailor's life. It permeated his clothes, his food, his possessions and even his sleep. Water poured over the forecastle as the ship ploughed her way through the sea, running along the deck and cascading into the well deck like a waterfall. It also surged inboard over the low gunwale of the maindeck and through the washports along the side. The maindeck was wet even on calm days, and in the early Canadian corvettes the absence of "Semtex" non-slip deck covering made simple walking hazardous. Manhandling 420-lb depth charges into their throwers on a heaving, slippery deck was difficult and dangerous work. From the maindeck, water seeped into the interior of the ship through countless passageways, ventilators and hatches. At action stations it was necessary to rig a block-and-tackle assembly down hatches running through the forward messdecks to the magazine in the bowels of the ship. This allowed water to pour directly into crew's accommodation. Dampness, cold weather, and the heat of huddled bodies produced condensation on the deckheads and fittings. The torrent of water on the deck was thus matched by a steady stream of water dripping from above. In the early days condensation ran along the deckheads and wiring into electrical panels and junction boxes, which novice Canadian shipbuilders had laid out like a home electrical application with the wires coming in from the top, and shorting them out. Once wet, sailors often stayed wet for the balance of

the crossing—two weeks or more. Bathing was out of the question and so corvette sailors and messdecks had a pungent odour to them after weeks at sea. The final indignity of the first corvettes was the straight pipe that ran from the ships' toilets to the sea. Timing was everything.

Not surprisingly then, most corvette sailors remember their time at sea as one of numbing fatigue and constant discomfort. In 1941 the situation was particularly trying since many essentials, such as foul-weather gear and duffle coats, were in short supply. In some corvettes there was just enough foul-weather clothing for one watch. The coats had to be exchanged as the watch changed and they stayed wet until they dried in the wind. Other shortfalls in basic equipment included telescopes (essential for reading flag signals at long distance) or even binoculars, and basic signalling equipment such as 20-inch signal projectors. In the absence of the latter, in 1941 most Canadian corvettes carried small hand-held Aldis lamps which lacked range and were inadequate for most North Atlantic conditions. Even sufficient refrigeration for more than a few days was lacking. For the first year corvette crews of NEF survived on a diet of hard tack and pickled beef— the fare of Nelson's navy, but the only diet that would endure the rigours of corvette life in the North Atlantic.

The sailors too were utterly unprepared for operations in the North Atlantic. In the summer of 1941 eighty percent of most corvette crews were new to the sea, with only a handful of key ratings experienced in the operation of weapons and equipment. Most officers too were novices, and in many corvettes the only qualified watchkeeper—and the only one capable of rudimentary navigation—was the captain himself. Many of the first captains were old salts of the merchant service, hearty and skilled sailors, unimpressed by naval discipline and ill-suited to the pressures of modern naval warfare. In time they were replaced by young Volunteer Reservists enlisted and trained for wartime service. Corvettes were, after all, young men's ships. In terms of simple safety at sea, corvette crews in this first year of the war were—as Commodore Murray, commander of NEF observed—dependant upon the ability of the captain to stay awake for weeks on end. One RN officer commented derisively in the fall of 1941 that "Canadian corvettes are suitable only for rescue work." There are few instances of men and ships going to war so ill prepared.

*The result of considerable effort: depth charge and its carrier leaving **Pictou's** aft portside thrower in March 1942. Note that the wooden deck covering on the quarterdeck does not extend to the depth charge throwers, and that the deck itself is awash.*

*Checking out ditty-bags in the seamen's mess of **Battleford**, alongside at Sydney, November 1941: quite comfortable, not yet overcrowded and still rather tidy.*

Battleford from the outside in November 1941. Americans who saw corvettes at work in the North Atlantic wondered why their crews did not get submarine pay, and Battleford at speed suggests why they thought so.

Nonetheless, they did so, and with enthusiasm. It helped that the close escorts were not really expected to defeat the attacks on convoys single-handed. Routing of convoys away from danger areas identified by naval intelligence was the principal means of defending shipping. The object of the escort was to provide a deterrent and defence against U-boat attack and to ensure the "safe and timely" arrival of the convoy. To do this, the NEF was organized into escort groups, each initially including three corvettes and one destroyer, patterned on the British system. The size of these groups would grow through the latter half of 1941 until, by early 1942, the operational strength of each group was four to five corvettes and two destroyers. What forced the increase in size was a series of bitter convoy battles fought in the NEF's area of operations, and largely involving the NEF, in September and October 1941. By that time the USN had been drawn into escort of convoy operations west of Iceland, alongside the Canadians based at St John's. Under a joint British-American agreement reached in August, the area west of Iceland was declared a "non-war zone" and the USN developed plans to escort convoys there under the guise of neutrality. Since the American escort force deployed to the North Atlantic was composed of destroyers, it was agreed that the USN would escort the fast convoys (9 to 14.9 knots) while the Canadian escorts of NEF—largely corvettes—escorted the slow convoys (7 to 8.9 knots).

It was Canadian-escorted slow convoys that bore the brunt of German wolf pack attacks in the North Atlantic in late 1941, and again a year later. The most dramatic of these 1941 actions, and one of the great battles of the war, was that for SC.42 in September. This slow convoy of sixty-four merchant ships in twelve columns was escorted by Escort Group 24: the destroyer *Skeena*, with the senior officer of the group, Cdr J. Hibbard, RCN, aboard, and the corvettes *Orillia*, *Alberni*, and *Kenogami*. Apart from *Kenogami*, the group had sailed together several times before. Operating in support of convoys in the Cape Farewell, Greenland, area were two other RCN corvettes of a training group under Chummy Prentice, his own *Chambly*, and the new corvette *Moose Jaw*.

The routing for SC.42 took the convoy through the gap between land-based air support to the northeast,

*A unique shot: **Lévis** sinking astern of convoy SC.44 in September 1941, her bows all but severed by U 74's torpedo. Corvettes normally sank too fast to have their photos taken after suffering fatal damage.*

*The Revised Patrol Vessels of the 1940-1941 program embodied many improvements, such as the extended forecastle displayed by **Halifax** at Collingwood in September 1941.*

along the east coast of Greenland, to skirt a waiting U-boat pack, and then east roughly along the latitude of Iceland. As it altered course from northeast to east, the convoy came under attack by a pack of fourteen U-boats for two nights, during which EG-24 fought essentially alone. In the darkness of the arctic night, the small escort screen was unable to detect U-boats as they penetrated the convoy to launch their torpedoes. The first attack, which began just before midnight on 9 September, was typical for the period and hit SC.42 shortly after it altered course to the east. The convoy was making 5 knots in a moderate sea, with a strong wind from the east-southeast, and a nearly full moon had just risen to the south. Skeena was ahead of the centre column of the convoy, Kenogami was portside escort, Alberni to starboard and Orillia astern. The first attack hit a ship in the outside port column—directly adjacent to Kenogami. The ship, laden with iron ore, disappeared beneath the sea almost immediately, leaving Kenogami no reference point from which to begin her search for the attacker. Nonetheless, after briefly pursuing a false sonar contact, the corvette's crew sighted a U-boat on the surface and Kenogami gave chase. Since the corvette still lacked a powerful searchlight or even illumination rounds (starshell) for her 4-inch gun, she got only one shot off at the U-boat before the firing of the main gun—which also lacked flashless powder—night-blinded the crew and the U-boat escaped. Skeena soon arrived to help, firing illuminants all around, but was immediately called away to the head of the convoy as another U-boat was reported. An hour and a half after the first attack ships in the ninth column of the convoy reported a U-boat on the surface. Skeena turned back from her position ahead and made speed down between the seventh and eighth columns. As she did so the convoy commodore ordered an emergency turn, intended to foil the enemy. Skeena thus found herself steering to avoid a collision with ships in the convoy just as the U-boat passed her, heading up the convoy lanes and drawing fire from all sides. In the midst of this hectic action two ships were torpedoed, and fell out of station astern of the convoy. Searches revealed little, but Orillia remained astern to rescue survivors and subsequently stayed behind to salvage the stricken tanker Tahchee. That removed a quarter of the escort from the action.

Two suspense-filled hours then passed before another attack on the portside sent Kenogami and Skeena off on further searches. At that moment

Alberni's turn came with the first attack on the starboard side. Unable to locate the attacker herself, Alberni too soon turned to rescue work. By the end of the first night SC.42 had been attacked successfully four times, losing several ships with no known retribution exacted from the enemy. Two further ships were lost during the day on the tenth.

As attacks developed on SC.42, Prentice and his two ships worked their way toward the stricken convoy, but could not arrive before the second evening. Prentice planned to make the best of his late arrival by approaching the convoy from the dark side—the same side used by the U-boats—in hopes of finding an attacker silhouetted against the moonlit horizon and with his attention focused on the convoy ahead. This is precisely what occurred. As Chambly and Moose Jaw closed with SC.42, and just as the pyrotechnics of the second night of battle illuminated the sky ahead of the two corvettes, Chambly's sonar operator got a firm contact. The range was just 700 yards, well inside the prescribed minimum range of 1200 yards for the commencement of a depth charge attack. "In view of the handiness and small turning circle of a corvette," Prentice wrote in his report, "it was decided to attack at once." At that point Prentice slowed the corvette down and, once the attack was lined up, a pattern of five depth charges was fired—just two minutes after the initial contact. All five charges exploded and when Chambly turned to renew her contact, U 501 surfaced alongside Moose Jaw as that corvette passed through the scene of the attack. The U-boat was so close to Moose Jaw that her captain stepped from his own conning tower onto the forecastle of the corvette. Moose Jaw, prepared to "repel boarders," veered away, rammed the submarine, and then swept German sailors away from their deck gun with machine-gun fire as they attempted to hit back. As Moose Jaw drifted away from the U-boat, Chambly came alongside and sent a boarding party onto a sinking U 501. One of the corvette's crew, trapped inside, went with the submarine on her final plunge to the bottom of the Atlantic.

Prentice's attack on U 501 reflected his belief that the corvette was a match for a U-boat if handled aggressively and with skill. Existing procedure called for attacks on submerged submarines to begin at about 1200 yards, closing to a throw-off point 800 yards from the contact. At that point speed was increased to close the distance and intercept the submarine along its anticipated path, at which time the depth charges were fired. The increase in speed was intended to close the distance to the firing point quickly, and so reduce the likelihood of effective evasion by the submarine. At the same time, the speed carried the corvette clear of the shock of its own depth charges. The problem of the increase in speed and the distance between the throw-off and firing points was that U-boats could hear the changing pitch of the escort's propeller and take evasive action. The increased speed also drowned out the ship's sonar, and so the final approach was entirely blind. Prentice believed that the corvette's short turning radius of 400 yards permitted—and the limitations of the Type 123A Asdic demanded—more resolute action. He advocated a steady attack speed of 12 knots, which was also the best search speed, and a closer throw-off point of 400 yards. In short, more deliberation, less rushing around. Theoretically, such a procedure allowed for a series of quick and accurate attacks. The drawbacks, not evident in the attack on *U 501* but experienced in later actions around SC.42, were serious. The slow attack speed advocated by Prentice was further reduced by the use of the helm at the throw-off point, which cut the actual speed of the ship by the time it reached the firing point. At slow speeds the potential for major damage to the corvette from its own depth charges was real: *Chambly's* electrical system was blown and the engine room crewmen shaken by the force of her own explosions later in the battle for SC.42. It is conceivable that many of the early complaints about faulty workmanship in the first corvettes were actually the result of this enthusiastic depth charge procedure.

The attacks on SC.42 went on for a second night with further losses—fifteen ships in all before it was finished. The corvettes performed well enough, but they and their crews were no match for a wolf pack attack. The battles around SC.44, SC.48 and SC.52 produced fewer losses, but overall the results achieved by NEF escort groups in late 1941 were poor. Apart from the obvious need to train the men and officers, work the groups together as teams and work out sensible operational plans, the ships themselves needed new equipment for their new role. Some form of radar to detect the U-boats on the surface at night was essential, and an early Canadian set, the SW1C, developed by the National Research Council from a British design, was being fitted as the year came to an end. The SW1C (and its later variant the SW2C) was a

1.5-metre wavelength set. Its "yagi" antenna, which resembled postwar television antennas, was fitted at the masthead atop a support rod which ran down the back of the mast. The rod carried the radar cable and was itself attached to a mechanism that allowed the antenna to be rotated. The cable and a directing linkage ran from the mast into the officers' toilet on the forward portside of the deckhouse, which was converted into the radar room. Like the sonar transducer below, the SW1C antenna had to be trained by the operator by means of a handwheel, producing a very slow sweep. Full 360-degree radar coverage around a SW1C-equipped ship was largely impractical, and operators tended to sweep only threatened sectors. Moreover, although the long wavelength (1.5 metres) was sufficient for navigational purposes, the SW1C was a failure in an anti-submarine role since it could not easily detect a surfaced U-boat in moderate or heavy seas. However, the SW2C (which had an improved cable linking the antenna to the set) was retained until 1944 because of its value as an aircraft warning set.

Operations in the Atlantic also revealed that Canadian-built corvettes had a particular penchant to rust. Professional naval officers, especially British ones, put this down to sloppy discipline among Canada's wartime sailors. In fact, it was a defect built into the ships as a result of hasty wartime building. The problem was mill scale: that layer of grime left on the face of steel plate after it has been rolled. The normal practice was either to send the steel to a "pickling plant" where the mill scale was removed, or to stack it outside and let the weather take effect. The latter was the preferred method in Canada, since the country had only two pickling plants, but the steel was stacked so tightly and used so quickly that the mill scale was still in place when the primer and final paint were applied. A few weeks of wind and salt air removed the scale, and with it all the protection for the steel. In the fall and winter of 1941 Canada's corvette fleet, demonstrably incapable of defending convoys from determined attackers, also had to battle built-in rust.

The poor appearance of the NEF over the winter of 1941/42 drew critical comments from American as well as British officers at the time, and stayed with the RCN thereafter. The Canadian navy's harshest postwar critic, Captain Donald Macintyre, RN, who served in Newfoundland over that first winter, wrote a scathing condemnation of NEF in his wartime memoir *U-Boat Killer*. But problems with the expansion fleet went much deeper than paint and mill scale. There were so many Canadian corvettes alongside at St John's for repairs by the end of 1941 that senior American and British officers wondered seriously if the RCN could maintain its commitment to ocean escort of convoys. Fortunately, after November 1941 the U-boats were busy elsewhere for a considerable period.

The first year of operations was not without losses, and these demonstrated the vulnerability of the tiny ships. They were, after all, not designed to withstand heavy damage. Most of the forward portion was crew space, and the boiler and engine room spaces were wide open from the keel to the skylight. One torpedo hit was enough. On 19 September *Lévis* was struck by a torpedo from *U 74* while escorting SC.44. The explosion severed the forward portion of the ship, killing seventeen men outright. The crippled ship remained afloat for over five hours, but then suddenly listed and sank. Forty survivors were recovered. The second loss resulted from a collision on 7 December when the freighter *Zypenberg* struck *Windflower* in a Grand Banks fog. The inrush of cold sea water blew up one of the corvette's boilers, throwing overboard the starboard boat and several crewmen. The explosion was heard by ships nearby, and it was initially thought that *Windflower* had been torpedoed. Forty-seven of her crew were rescued, three of whom later died.

On the day that *Windflower* was lost, a greater tragedy was unfolding in the Pacific. As a handful of young Canadians perished in the Atlantic, Japanese bombs and torpedoes sent over 2,000 young Americans and the pride of the US Pacific Fleet to the bottom of Pearl Harbor. It was an event which would, in the end, draw Canadian corvettes back to more placid inshore waters, spread them throughout the North Atlantic, and rob them of the opportunity to adapt to the new kind of Atlantic war. It was nonetheless fitting that as 1941 drew to a close the Admiralty's Director of Anti-Submarine Warfare sent a note of apology to the NEF's commander, observing that British assessment of NEF operations over the fall had been "far too critical." And so they had. Although neither the ships or the men were prepared for the requirements of modern war, their mere presence had permitted the establishment of the escorted convoy system upon which the defence of Allied shipping rested. This too would be the story of 1942.

*Looking down on the forward portion of the revised corvette **Woodstock** at Collingwood, 30 March 1942. Her forecastle deck extending to the funnel shows clearly on the right side of the photo and her bridge shows signs of developing into something useful.*

CHAPTER III

New Roles, Modified Designs And Operations In 1942

The lessons of the fall of 1941, including the urgent need to rebuild the original corvettes to suit their new role in the mid-Atlantic, had little time to take hold in the RCN before the Japanese attack on Pearl Harbor radically changed the nature of the war. In this desperate new phase ships of all types were badly needed. During 1942 the Canadian corvette fleet was pushed to its limit, as the RCN undertook escort operations ranging throughout the north and central Atlantic, into the Mediterranean, and to the Aleutian Islands in the North Pacific. Although many classes of ships were pressed into service to give the RCN such unprecedented reach, what really made it possible were the ships of the 1939-1940 and 1940-1941 corvette building programs. They became, in 1942, the core of the nation's naval effort. In the process, the ships were run hard, and most attempts to remedy the shortcomings in basic design evident from the 1941 experience could not be undertaken.

At the end of 1941 most of the RCN's corvettes were concentrated in the Newfoundland Escort Force: indeed the emphasis of the RCN's war at that point was to the north and east of Newfoundland. With official American entry into the war, U-boats began to look at her unprotected eastern seaboard, and in January 1942 the first German submarines appeared off Nova Scotia and New England. Their attacks were not unexpected, but the level of American unpreparedness came as a rude shock to everyone, as did the USN's reluctance to begin immediately a system of coastal convoys. The pull of the war in the Atlantic in early 1942 was therefore south and west, as the Germans probed deeper into American waters. And as disaster followed disaster for the Allies in the Pacific more ships were needed to stem the Japanese tide. With the shifting weight of the war went most—indeed virtually all—of the USN forces serving alongside the NEF.

By February 1942 it was necessary to reorganize the trans-Atlantic escort system. The RCN forces of the Newfoundland Escort Force and UK-based RN ships abandoned Iceland as an ocean meeting point for the exchange of escort duties and combined their efforts into a single Mid Ocean Escort Force. The new MOEF was responsible for the escort of trade convoys between the Grand Banks and UK waters—a long, open stretch of ocean. The limited range of both destroyers and corvettes while on escort duty forced these convoys to stay close to the most direct route, the Great Circle Route, during most of 1942. In the first part of 1942 convoys transiting the air gap in the mid-ocean, what

Training for the new war against the wolf packs required teamwork, some help from tame submarines to play the enemy, motor launches to represent the convoy, and air cover: all elements displayed in this December 1941 shot of corvettes exercising off Halifax. The submarine is Free Dutch.

the Germans called the Black Pit, were largely free from wolf pack attacks. Therefore the comparatively small size of MOEF groups and their predictable routing were not causes for serious concern.

MOEF group composition changed over the year, but as a rule authorities attempted to ensure that two destroyers and four to five corvettes escorted each convoy through the air gap. Throughout most of 1942 MOEF had eleven such groups: nominally, four RCN, six RN and one USN. Within the Canadian groups there was the equivalent of one RN group on loan, usually concentrated in group C-2. USN involvement in convoy escort in the North Atlantic dwindled rapidly in 1942, until by April it was down to a single token group, A-3. The core of the group was normally the large, but slow Hamilton Class Coast Guard cutters, buttressed by the occasional aged USN destroyer. A-3's numbers were usually topped up with Canadian corvettes. The six British groups of the MOEF also contained many ships manned by European navies-in-exile, and one of the

best RN groups, B-6, had a superb core of Norwegian-manned corvettes.

Thus the MOEF was a multi-national escort force, and heavily dependent on corvettes. But RN corvettes in MOEF by 1942 had been at least partially modernized, both structurally and in equipment. This modernization program extended to the nine remaining British corvettes operated by the RCN. Between December 1941 and early March 1942, five of these corvettes—Arrowhead, Bittersweet, Eyebright, *Mayflower* and *Snowberry*—went to Charleston, South Carolina, to refit. Their forecastles were extended, bridges improved, heavier secondary armament fitted, sonar improved and modern Type 271 radar fitted. Two other ships received similar treatment from American yards in 1942, *Trillium* in the spring and *Fennel* in the late summer. As a result, these were the best-equipped corvettes in the RCN during the crisis in the Atlantic war; unfortunately, not all of them were where the action was.

RCN corvettes began to discard their battleship grey for light- disruptive camouflage schemes, designed to make them harder to see at night, in the winter of 1941-1942. **Algoma,** *her new paint the worse for wear, is seen here steaming up the Foyle River to Londonderry sometime in early 1942.*

Of the other two British corvettes in Canadian service, one, *Hepatica*, was not modernized until 1943. The other, *Spikenard*, never had the opportunity. She was lost on the night of 10 February while escorting convoy SC.67 south of Iceland. It was a particularly dark night, with a high sea running, and *Spikenard* was on station—alone—on the starboard wing of the convoy. About eleven o'clock *U 136* fired two torpedoes toward the convoy. The first struck a nearby tanker and the second, almost simultanously, struck *Spikenard* between the bridge and forecastle. The explosion ripped the side away from the ship and started a raging fire. Men emerging from the forward messdecks had to run a gauntlet of flames, some falling into the gaping hole in the corvette's deck. In five minutes she was gone, and as *Spikenard* settled in the water, another explosion, either from a boiler or a depth charge, smashed the remaining boat and one of the Carley floats. Meanwhile, the stricken tanker burned and drew the attention of the escort. By the time the first corvette arrived on the scene, *Spikenard* was gone without anyone noticing. It was only at dawn the next morning that the corvette was noticed missing. The British corvette *Gentian* was sent back to look and early in the afternoon, more than fourteen hours after the torpedoing, eight of *Spikenard*'s crew—all who were ever found—were rescued.

Apart from changes in paint scheme to the new light disruptive patterns, and a few modest structural improvements to extend the bridge wings and add crew comforts where possible, RCN corvettes remained largely unaltered during 1942. Consequently, they were the weakest link in the MOEF chain. Their overall performance was also exacerbated by the distribution of duties within the new MOEF. Although there is no evidence of a formal agreement, under the MOEF system, the RCN continued to escort the vast majority of the slow convoys, while the RN groups escorted fast ones. Since the speed with which convoys crossed the air gap or moved away from shadowing U-boats was crucial to their loss rates, fate dealt the RCN a hard hand in 1942.

The reorganization of escort tasks in February also brought new form to Canadian local escort arrangements. Halifax-based escorts, now more important than ever, gained increased status as the Western Local Escort Force. Short-ranged Canadian, British and Norwegian destroyers were diverted to help WLEF, and in May the RCN's new Bangor class minesweepers—also limited to less than 3,000 miles' range—were assigned to escort duty in WLEF as well.

As the year wore on and German depredations spread, the RCN was forced to extend its escort duties. Convoys linking Boston with the major assembly port of Halifax were begun at the end of March.

As noted below, demands on Canadian escort resources grew dramatically throughout 1942, but few of these new commitments could be met by new-construction corvettes. With the exception of *Moncton*, commissioned in April 1942, all of the original 1939-1940 building program were in service by the end of 1941. So too were five of the 1940-1941 program; the balance of this batch, eleven ships, commissioned in the first half of 1942. The total of new corvettes between January and June 1942, twelve in all, was utterly inadequate to meet the new operational demands. Some of the shortfall would be made up by using other types of ships. It was inevitable, however, that many of the nearly seventy corvettes based in Newfoundland would be called away. The reduction of corvette strength in Newfoundland began in March when five were transferred to Halifax. Three more followed in April. There were further reductions, and many ships sent to Nova Scotia for refit found themselves reassigned to other tasks when the yards were finished.

By May 1942, losses to shipping along the US east coast were so grave that the RCN began to escort Canadian oil tanker convoys to and from the Caribbean: only corvettes had the range for that task. These convoys operated until late August/early September, by which time the US east coastal convoy system was established. It was while on one of the last of these tanker operations on 28 August that the corvette *Oakville* blew *U 94* to the surface, swept her decks with gunfire, rammed her twice and then sent Sub Lt H. Lawrence and Petty Officer A. J. Powell away as a boarding party. Lawrence has immortalized the incident in his memoir *A Bloody War*. The corvettes assigned to tanker duties, essentially *Oakville*, *Snowberry*, *Sudbury*, *The Pas*, and the revised corvettes *Halifax* and *Fredericton*, were transferred to the USN's Commander Eastern Sea Frontier in September and sailed the New York-Guantanamo Bay route until the spring of 1943.

The drain of corvettes from the mid-ocean peaked again in June and July 1942, when sixteen ships left the trans-Atlantic routes for inshore work. At least one of these MOEF ships, *Lethbridge*, joined other corvettes in an intense battle right under the noses of Canadians at home. In July German attacks in the Gulf of St

Lawrence and in the river itself forced the RCN to establish convoys between Quebec City and Sydney. Among the collection of ships—armed yachts, motor launches, Bangors, old destroyers—assigned to the Gulf Escort Force were five corvettes, including *Arrowhead*. One of them, the revised corvette *Charlottetown*, was sunk by two torpedoes from *U 517* off the Gaspé on the morning of 11 September. The torpedoes caused few casualties, but *Charlottetown*'s crew had only three minutes to abandon ship before she disappeared, and when she did a depth charge exploded, killing six men in the water and wounding several others. In all fifty-five of her crew survived.

New-construction corvettes from Canadian yards poured into these new operations as well, so that by midsummer most of the RCN's corvette strength was operating south and west of the Grand Banks. Although except for *U 94* no U-boat was sunk by the RCN in these operations, and many ships were lost to enemy action particularly in the Gulf, convoy and escort arrangements cobbled together by the RCN in the western Atlantic during 1942 were highly successful. Their purpose was not to defeat the German attack by aggressive means, and certainly not to stop the U-boats by sinking them. Rather, the convoy and escort system complicated the German submariners' problems of location and attack of targets just enough to make most of his inshore operations at this stage of the war unprofitable—and it got the shipping through. The system made the German search problem harder by clearing the sea of many easy targets and, through use of intelligence, safely routing convoys well away from danger areas. Since the Germans were unable to use wolf packs inshore because of Allied airpower, it was difficult for individual U-boats to find a convoy, especially on the wide coastal convoy lanes. If a U-boat captain did find a convoy, he could expect to get in one good attack before oppressive surface and air patrols made life difficult for him. Since U-boats still needed to run on the surface to recharge their batteries, lingering in the approaches to harbours was considered unwise. The only place where the German inshore campaign achieved a marked success against coastal convoys was in the River and Gulf of St Lawrence. Here the narrowness of the river and the channel between Cape Gaspé and Anticosti Island made location of convoys comparatively easy, while the mixing of fresh and sea water made sonar conditions notoriously bad. In the end, the RCN was forced to abandon the Gulf convoys in September 1942 and close the waterway to ocean shipping for the balance of that year and most of the next.

In the same month the assembly port for trans-Atlantic convoys moved from Nova Scotia to New York. This brought the reorganization of the WLEF into two relays, north of Halifax and south of Halifax, to accommodate the short range of the old destroyers and the Bangors. These escort groups were often quite small in comparison to those of the MOEF, but they faced a much lower level of enemy activity. The typical WLEF group consisted of one destroyer, one Bangor class minesweeper and two corvettes. They shuttled doggedly along what was called the Triangle Run: New York, Halifax and St John's. It was unspectacular duty. Perhaps its only major distinction was the severity of the winter weather. The waters off Nova Scotia and Newfoundland, where the Labrador current snaked along the coast, were the coldest of any in the Atlantic except the North Russia route. Most of the MOEF's operations, although unpleasant enough, followed the northern reaches of the Gulf Stream. WLEF faced bitterly cold arctic seas and weather patterns. Heavy ice build-up on ships in winter was a major cause of instability—and anxiety. For these reasons, when the RCN considered the matter of "arcticizing" its ships later in the war, those based at Halifax got priority.

Canada's hastily built and poorly equipped corvettes were equal to the task of inshore escort in 1942 because they served their primary purpose by simply being there. Although the Naval Staff was sharply criticized at the end of 1943 for failing to begin modernization of its corvette fleet in 1942 (the subject of the next chapter), and the Chief of the Naval Staff was ultimately fired, it was clearly the right decision at the time. The RCN did allow itself the luxury of setting aside the new corvette *Kitchener* for a month (during her workups) in mid-1942 for the filming of *Corvette K-225*, Hollywood's salute to the small-ship navy. With the great American star of western films, Randolph Scott, riding herd on the convoys from the bridge of his corvette, *Corvette K-225* manages to settle the score with the fiendish Hun with all the aplomb wartime propaganda could muster. Despite that, and although clearly not the classic film about corvettes (Nicholas Monsarrat's *The Cruel Sea* takes that honour), *Corvette K-225* is a fitting memento of the the days when corvettes carried the burden of the war.

Whether the final commitment of Canadian corvettes in August 1942 to yet another operation, this time in the eastern Atlantic and Mediterranean, was warranted is perhaps open to more critical comment. Allied planners decided in July 1942 to begin their offensive operations against Germany with an amphibious assault on North Africa, Operation Torch. The RCN was asked to provide as many escorts as possible at a time when it was already stretched to the limit. By withdrawing all but *Dawson* and *Vancouver* (who sailed in August to participate in the Aleutian campaign) from the west coast, replacing seven in the WLEF with Bangors and withdrawing all corvettes from the Gulf Escort Force, the RCN sent seventeen corvettes to the Torch landings. The first six sailed for Britain on 10 September and participated in the actual assault; the balance sailed through October and November to work with the supporting forces. Before leaving Canada or upon their arrival in the UK, the Torch corvettes were equipped with four 20-mm Oerlikon guns in new platforms abreast the engine room casing and modern 10-cm surface warning radar. Significantly, six of the nine remaining revised corvettes—*Calgary, Kitchener, Port Arthur, Regina, Ville de Québec*, and *Woodstock*—were assigned to Torch. With *Halifax* and *Fredericton* already on loan to the USN, that left *La Malbaie* as the only revised patrol vessel to serve in the mid-Atlantic in the winter of 1942-1943. Of the partially modernized—but quite well equipped—British corvettes in RCN service, four of the seven (*Bittersweet, Eyebright, Mayflower*, and *Trillium*) served with the MOEF during late 1942 and early 1943, two (*Arrowhead* and *Fennel*) were assigned to the WLEF, and *Snowberry* was on loan to the USN. Thus, whether by accident or design most of the best of the RCN's corvettes and its best equipped were on loan to other navies by the fall of 1942.

The dispersion of the RCN escort strength through early 1942 and the allocation of some of the most modern ships to foreign navies was perhaps unavoidable. Until the middle of the year the action was certainly much hotter elsewhere, and the Germans largely set the tempo of the war in the Atlantic. But the consequences for the RCN, in the end, were great. Ships sailed on without refits, without new equipment, without essential repairs, without boiler cleanings, and without proper training. For those operating inshore this neglect mattered little, either to their convoys or to the reputation of the RCN. However, for the escort groups facing wolf packs in the mid-Atlantic air gap the quality

*Only a few months into her career, but already showing the effects of North Atlantic wear and tear: **Algoma** with a convoy in 1941.*

*Winter meant ice buildup often enough to paralyze the weapons and affect the stability of the ship. **Lunenburg's** depth charge equipment remains well frozen-in, but her twin .50-calibre machine guns at least have been freed.*

of their twenty-five remaining Canadian corvettes was crucial, and the price of such neglect was high.

By the middle of the year the Germans began to move back into the mid-Atlantic air gap in appreciable numbers, as the extension of Allied convoy systems reduced their success rates in distant theatres. As they did so the Germans found the Allies sailing close to the Great Circle Route along predictable paths and with slightly reduced escort groups. Allied land-based airpower still reached only about four hundred miles from Newfoundland and six hundred miles from Iceland and Britain into the Atlantic, so wolf packs could still operate with impunity in the mid-ocean against what now appeared to be easier targets.

The new phase of the mid-Atlantic battle began in July around two westbound, Canadian-escorted convoys. The first of these, ON.113, was not seriously challenged and the Canadian destroyer *St. Croix* of group C-2 sank *U 90* in the process. On the day that the U-boats lost contact with ON.113 they obtained contact with ON.115 as it entered the air gap west of Ireland. ON.115's escort, C-3, was very good, perhaps the best of the Canadian groups in the MOEF during 1942. Its corvette core, *Sackville*, *Galt*, and *Wetaskiwin*, underwent special training together in May off Newfoundland under Chummy Prentice in *Chambly*. During one of the exercises, *Sackville* and *Chambly* nearly collided while pursuing the same sonar echo in a fog bank. Skilled ship handling saved both ships from collision as they attacked the contact from opposite directions at the same time. The balance of C-3 comprised two RCN destroyers, *Saguenay*, under Cdr D. C. Wallace, RCNR, who was also senior officer of the group, and *Skeena*, commanded by Lt Cdr K. L. Dyer, RCN, who would later become an admiral. Altogether, it was an exceptional group and it enjoyed remarkable stability until late 1942.

Augmented by the corvette *Louisburg*, C-3 endured a number of alarms, false underwater contacts and mysterious medium frequency wireless transmissions, but the first few days passed uneventfully. Finally on 29 July *U 210*, on passage to the US, sighted ON.115: it took a day for the pack to assemble. On the thirtieth, while in the midst of the air gap, C-3 began to make U-boat sightings. Aggressive patrolling at visual range from the convoy during the day kept the pack off balance and only one U-boat closed during the night to attack. It was intercepted by *Skeena*. She and *Wetaskiwin*, in a textbook example of a combined hunt and attack,

destroyed the submarine, *U 558*, the next morning. Good sonar conditions had allowed the ships to retain contact with the U-boat and the two escorts took turns directing each other over the target.

By 31 July C-3 had managed to keep the pack at bay and destroy a U-boat, and on 1 August the Germans lost contact. C-3 had won the first round, but its efforts had reduced fuel in the destroyers to minimum and they left for St John's, while *Wetaskiwin* never did relocate the convoy after her battle with *U 558*. On 1-2 August 1942, defence of ON.115 briefly fell to the three remaining corvettes, *Galt*, *Louisburg*, and *Sackville*: a development which fortunately coincided with a gap in German contact. The corvette *Agassiz* joined the afternoon of 2 August, as did the destroyers *Witch* and *Hamilton*.

By the end of the day on 2 August C-3 was a scratch team, but it should not have mattered since they were within range of land-based air support. Unfortunately, fog prevented the aircraft from supporting ON. 115 and the U-boats of a new group made contact. At one hour before midnight, as ON.115 sailed westward, *Sackville* obtained an underwater contact on the port bow of the convoy. *Hamilton* left the convoy to assist, but by the time she arrived, Alan Easton, *Sackville*'s commanding officer, had determined the contact was a false one and the two escorts returned. Shortly thereafter the convoy commodore reported a U-boat inside the convoy and moments later two ships, *Lochkatrine* and *G. S. Walden*, were torpedoed. As the two stricken ships fell astern of the convoy, C-3 conducted Operation Raspberry, a standard search for the attacker with the escort using starshell and the merchant ships firing Snowflake rockets. As *Sackville* made her way back to ON.115 following the search, she came upon *Agassiz* and *Hamilton* taking survivors from the two sinking ships. Easton decided to screen the rescue work, and forty minutes later obtained a contact on a U-boat with *Sackville*'s SW1C radar. Calm conditions and a bit of luck worked in *Sackville*'s favour.

A contact on a SW1C set provided enough information to head toward the target, but not enough definition to provide its course and speed, or its identity. Final classification of the contact had to be done visually, and that delay eliminated much of the tactical advantage that later—better—radars provided. *Sackville* had to resort to illuminants to determine what her radar had uncovered, and, as the starshells burst, the clear profile of a U-boat emerged. A better radar would have uncovered secretly what the starshell now revealed, that the U-boat was slightly ahead and beam-on—an ideal position for ramming. However, the starshell warned the submariners, and before *Sackville* could completely close the distance, the U-boat had submerged. As the corvette raced over the swirl, expecting to strike some portion of the U-boat, a pattern of depth charges was fired. These charges blew the U-boat to the surface, her black bows pointing skyward, bathed in a plume of exploding sea. *Sackville*'s crew celebrated a kill: but the U-boat, badly shaken, survived. So did the others *Sackville* encountered that day.

Sackville searched the area for debris and attempted to regain contact, but neither search proved fruitful. After midnight fog closed in around the convoy and *Sackville*'s second contact of the night appeared again as another woolly blip on her radar. As the corvette probed her way through the foggy darkness, the blip finally transformed itself into another U-boat lying on the surface in an ideal position for ramming. However, once again the U-boat was able to dive faster than *Sackville* could close the distance to ram. No underwater contact was made, and Easton pointed his ship back toward ON.115.

The final contact of this hectic day came in the mid-afternoon of 3 August. *Sackville*'s return to the convoy was interrupted when she came upon *Agassiz*, now towing the damaged tanker *G. S. Walden*. Easton decided to screen *Agassiz* and her tow, and was rewarded for his thoughtfulness when *Sackville*'s sonar operator, using his set in a listening mode, picked up the sound of the U-boat's engines. Course alterations in the fog were made again by radar until finally visual contact was established. By then the U-boat was crossing *Sackville*'s bows two hundred yards ahead, from starboard to port, and making about 9 knots. Easton ordered "Hard a-port! Full ahead. Open fire!" as the U-boat moved past, but it was inside the corvette's turning circle and ramming was impossible. As *Sackville* heeled over in her hard turn to port and the distance closed, the 4-inch gun could be depressed enough to fire at point-blank range—"scarcely a ship's length away." The first shot struck the submarine's conning tower, ripping it open. The U-boat dived just as a second round passed over, while *Sackville*'s paltry secondary armament of Lewis and .50-calibre machine guns played harmlessly on the U-boat's thick pressure hull. Underwater contact was foiled by schools of fish, and the damaged U-boat escaped further detection.

Sackville's exploits on 2-3 August 1942 were exceptional: more excitement than most corvettes experienced in a whole war packed into a few short hours. But all three U-boats survived. Although Easton and his crew had done exceptionally well with the equipment they possessed, assessments at the time observed that *Sackville*'s U-boats "would have been a gift had she been fitted with RDF Type 271." *Sackville*'s contacts might well have been other escorts or ships from the convoys—or off Newfoundland even icebergs. Consequently, Easton had to pick his way carefully until the radar contacts could be confirmed by visual sightings, by which time it was too late for the corvette to act with the same speed as the diesel-driven U-boat. The modern British Type 271 radar, which was carried by most RN corvettes by 1942, operated on a 10-cm wavelength, and was sharp enough to have allowed *Sackville* to identify and plan her attack on the U-boats at night and in fog: a decisive advantage. Of course, modern radar would not have guaranteed the destruction of all three submarines since ramming usually severely damaged a corvette. *Sackville* might have been able to compensate for the lack of modern radar if she had had a heavier secondary armament of a 2-pdr or 20-mm Oerlikon guns with which to riddle the pressure hull of the U-boats, as did most of her British counterparts.

Most important, these equipment shortages also affected the ability of Canadian escorts to defend convoys adequately against attack during the latter half of 1942. The evidence of this is stark and simple: between July and the end of the year fully 80 percent of ships lost from convoys escorted by the MOEF's eleven groups came from those of the four C groups. The reasons for this are complex. The RCN's responsibility for the bulk of the vulnerable slow convoys was a major factor, and so, too, was the inability of the RCN to obtain any more long-range destroyers on short notice. Destroyers provided the tactical reach of MOEF groups. Their sweeps, directed by shipborne High Frequency Direction Finding (HF/DF) sets, which located the U-boats shadowing the convoy by picking up their sighting reports, could prevent the pack from assembling around the convoy. Corvettes were used occasionally for these sweeps, but they lacked the speed to catch U-boats on the surface and to return promptly to the convoy afterwards. Canadian escort groups also lacked the shipborne HF/DF sets through late 1942 (except for that fitted in *Restigouche*

In 1942 the RCN also expanded its operations closer to home and extended them south, to the US. To do that, it drew on its fleet of Bangor class minesweepers, which joined corvettes in an escort role. The difference between the two types is shown well here, as **La Malbaie** trails **Granby** during exercises in May 1942. Note they retain the grey overall paint scheme; Halifax- based escorts were slow to switch to light schemes, and new construction in 1942 still arrived in grey.

Sackville about the time of the battle for ON.115. Her equipment is typical of Canadian corvettes in 1942. She is still fitted with minesweeping gear, carries a light secondary armament (.50-calibre machine guns on the bridge wings, twin Lewis guns in the after gun position) and the Canadian 1.5-metre radar at the masthead.

*Operational demands in 1942 kept ships at sea when they should have been modernized. **Saskatoon**, seen here in 1942 or 1943, still has her original configuration, including the mainmast, although she has added radar atop the foremast and a "monkey island" on top of the charthouse.*

*British corvettes in Canadian service were partially modernized in the winter of 1941-1942: **Eyebright** about a year later is a study in contrasts with that of **Saskatoon** of the same period. The RCN badly needed the 20-mm secondary armament and the Type 271 radar (in the lantern behind the bridge) seen here.*

*The rest of **Eyebright** sometime in the winter of 1942-1943, showing her British heritage to good effect.*

*Corvettes destined for Operation Torch received additional firepower prior to leaving. **Kitchener**, awaiting departure in Halifax in September 1942, now carries a 2-pdr pom-pom in the after gun tub and four additional 20-mm Oerlikon guns on new extensions of the engine room casing deck.*

One of the very few photos taken of corvettes en route to Torch: a group of them stretched out across the Bay of Biscay from an unidentified ship. Note the ready-use ammunition for the Mk.IX gun.

of C-4). The later Castles were the only corvettes ever fitted with them.

If a MOEF group was unable to disrupt the development of a pack attack, its best option was a tight defence around the convoy based on modern Type 271 radar. The 271 set's 10-cm wavelength was not only sharp enough to classify U-boat contacts with considerable precision, but the set was also the first to sweep automatically and display the information in a "plan" on the screen, with the ship in the centre. The British ships in MOEF were fitted with 271 radar, as were the British corvettes on loan to the RCN. B groups therefore were able to detect U-boats attempting to enter the convoy at night. The SW1C and SW2C radars of Canadian ships lacked both the definition and the

sweeping capacity needed to establish and maintain a tight defence of a convoy at night.

The inability of the Canadian groups in MOEF to defend convoys adequately in 1942 was demonstrated in September during the battle for ON.127, a slow westbound convoy escorted by C-4. Seven merchant ships were lost, four damaged and the destroyer *Ottawa* sunk by the attackers. Of C-4's ships, the two RCN destroyers *Ottawa* and *St Croix*, and the corvettes *Amherst*, *Arvida*, *Sherbrooke*, and the RN corvette *Celandine*, only the British ship carried Type 271 radar. In the absence of good tactical intelligence from modern equipment, C-4's defence of ON.127 was haphazard, and the group did not inflict any apparent damage on the enemy. By contrast, the British-escorted ON.122, which passed through the gap in August, was heavily

The light disruptive camouflage schemes adopted by the RCN in 1942 had to be kept bright if they were to effectively reduce the ship's dark image on a night-time horizon. Keeping them bright was an endless task, as the painting party alongside **Kamsack** *in August 1942 could no doubt attest.*

attacked but lost only four ships. ON.122's escort, B-6, used its 271 radar to locate and drive off no fewer than thirteen U-boats as they closed the convoy at night to attack. No U-boat was destroyed, but the defence of the convoy was extremely well handled and losses to shipping much less than might have been expected.

The contrast between the well-equipped escorts of the B groups and the poor state of Canadian ships was demonstrated again in the fall—and again by B-6 and C-4. SC.104, a slow eastbound convoy escorted by B-6, was heavily attacked, losing eight ships early in its passage when bad weather affected radar efficiency. However, in moderating seas the escort recovered, punishing attackers as they closed the convoy and sinking two U-boats. C-4's crossing two weeks later with SC.107 cost the allies fifteen ships in exchange for no known U-boat losses. It was determined after the war that one U-boat was actually destroyed when a munitions ship in SC.107, which it had torpedoed, perished in one of the largest non-nuclear explosions ever. Shortly after SC.107, B-6 brought the slow convoy

ONS.144 through the air gap with only five corvettes as escorts. They held the U-boats to five merchant ships and managed to destroy one submarine in the exchange. The C groups of the MOEF, by all accounts, could neither attack or defend.

The British were quick to blame Canadian shortcomings on poor leadership and training, and by December 1942 were asking that the Canadian contribution to the MOEF be withdrawn. The RCN argued—rightly—that outdated equipment and a shortage of destroyers were at fault. The Canadian case was undermined by the dreadful passage of ONS.154 through the air gap in late December: sixteen ships lost and no apparent damage to the enemy (postwar assessments awarded the destruction of *U 356* to the escort, but there was no evidence of a successful attack at the time). The Canadians had no option but to agree to the withdrawal of their forces from the decisive theatre of the Atlantic war: the RCN and its jacks-of-all-trades had reached their limit.

CHAPTER IV

Modernization 1942-1944

The RCN was aware of British modifications to the basic corvette design while the bulk of the 1939-1940 program still lay in the builders' hands. Had the RCN been seriously concerned about the changing role or long-term purpose of their corvettes, it would have been possible to extend the forecastle and improve the bridges even before most of the ships were commissioned. Whether the RCN considered such action remains a mystery, but had they done so the ships would have been better suited to the longer patrols, larger crews and more active war that lay ahead. Moreover, the complexity of the modernization problem by 1943 would have been greatly reduced.

But, of course, hindsight is always perfect. For a number of reasons, then, the RCN failed to modernize its burgeoning corvette fleet in early 1941. Shipyards—unfamiliar with improvisation—were unable to work "off the back of an envelope" as experienced British yards could, although they might have been persuaded to do so had the navy decided to act. It did not. The ships themselves were urgently needed for operations, but just what kind of operations and where remained unclear in the fall of 1940. More important perhaps, it took a very long time for the RCN to identify corvettes as the basis of its war effort. As Commodore L. W. Murray, commander of the Newfoundland Escort Force, complained in late 1941, the Staff in Ottawa did not appreciate that "the reputation of the RCN in this war depends on the success or failure of the NEF..."—which meant, in large measure, the success or failure of its corvette fleet. Murray was right, but another year would pass before the Staff in Ottawa understood. Until the RCN itself gained operational experience with the ships, the clear need for the alterations would not be driven home.

A portion of the RCN corvette fleet actually began the modernization process during the winter of 1941-1942, but this owed nothing to Canadian action. Five of the British-owned corvettes in Canadian service underwent forecastle extension and bridge improvement in the winter of 1941-1942, at British expense in American yards. The RCN's own corvettes were not so fortunate. Discussions about new warship construction within the RCN in early 1942 indicate that Canadian authorities believed that the corvette—as a whole class of ship—was now obsolete. In fairness, this belief was shared by the British as well. While the RN put considerable effort into modernizing existing ships, by early 1942 they had all but abandoned corvette

Eyebright undergoing a partial modernization at Charleston, SC, in the winter of 1941-1942. Her forecastle extension has been framed, as have the extensions to her bridge wings, while the housing for the Type 271 radar is nearly completed behind the bridge. The small extension ahead of the bridge (with the workman on it) will carry the additional magnetic compass binnacle and bearing indicator needed to convert the Type 123A sonar to a Type 123D.

construction and were moving on to more advanced types such as Twin-Screw Corvettes, or what later became known as frigates. Already well behind in modernization, the dilemma faced by the RCN in early 1942 was whether to *start* the modernization of seventy ships now considered obsolete, or put their efforts into construction of entirely new types. Developments at sea complicated the issue. The requirement in early 1942, as commitments multiplied, was for ships of any type to expand the convoy systems that were the bedrock of Allied trade defence. As noted in Chapter III, the RCN responded enthusiastically to British and American calls for help, and in the process overextended its reach in 1942. If the RCN initially seemed hesitant to improve the corvette fleet, it was with good reason.

There were three essential requirements for the modernization of the first construction program corvettes:

1. Acquisition of the necessary equipment, particularly gyro compasses and the more modern sonar sets which went with them, newer types of weaponry coming into use such as 20-mm Oerlikons and ahead-throwing anti-submarine mortars like Hedgehog;
2. Major structural changes to the hull and bridge to improve seakeeping, accommodation and command arrangements;
3. The rewiring of the ship with the low-power system needed to operate both the Hedgehog, gyro compasses and the newer sonars.

Mayflower *showing very clearly the forecastle extension and "new" Type 271 radar lantern—which is actually of a very early pattern—fitted at Charleston, SC, in the winter of 1941-1942. Note, however, that her mast remains ahead of the bridge. Evidence of an American refit also shows on the heads of three crewmen.*

Apart from cutting and fitting the steel needed for structural changes, little of the modernization program was within easy grasp of the RCN in 1942 and 1943. The complexity of the task and the RCN's lack of direct control over the resources needed induced paralysis in the whole process. The desire to proceed with piecemeal modernization, either by partial structural improvements or the addition of crucial new equipment, conflicted with the ultimate need to rewire the ships with the low-power supply required for the Hedgehog, electronic plots, gyro compass and modern sonar. Rewiring entailed considerable time and work, and yet until it was completed, a piecemeal modernization was not practicable. Certainly there was little purpose in rebuilding the forward portion of the ship only to rip it apart later to rewire (although this is what happened to the British corvettes on loan to Canada). Far better if the whole effort could be completed in a single refit.

Some partial improvements, as explained below, such as modern radar and heavier secondary armament, were possible, but increasingly, the need was for accurate navigation, accurate anti-submarine searches and counterattacks on submerged targets. As the officer in charge of operational efficiency of St John's-based escorts observed in mid-1943, "The problems of a corvette captain when attempting an accurate attack with a swinging magnetic compass are well nigh insoluble." Until the wiring was done, little progress could be made in fitting modern electronic navigation, sonar, and plotting equipment.

Modernization was complicated by the fact that the RCN had no direct control over supplies of modern equipment, most of which came from the UK, or over the shipyards where the work could be carried out. The difficulties of access to Great Lakes and British Columbia yards have been mentioned. The latter could

*By 1943 no two RCN corvettes' bridges were alike, but they all desperately needed work—as **Alberni** amply demonstrates upon her arrival for modernization. Her poorly supported bridge wings, their .50-calibre machine guns removed from their mounts, are sagging badly.*

be reached after a long voyage, but the Ontario yards which built the bulk of the corvette fleet were inaccessible to the ships once they were fitted out and ballasted for service. By 1942 east coast yards were either overworked or neglected. The big shipyards of Halifax and Saint John were crowded and busy with work, largely for civilian agencies. The small yards, upon which the navy relied for its rudimentary annual refits of small vessels, were never part of the government's industrial plans for the war and were not seen by the RCN as important to its long-term maintenance requirements. Although new shipyards sprouted like mushrooms around the Great Lakes in 1940-1941, none appeared in Atlantic Canada and only three ships—*Amherst*, *Moncton* and *Sackville*—were completed for the RCN in the Maritimes before the end of the war. Shipyard services outside of Halifax and Saint John were understaffed, poorly equipped and badly coordinated. In short, Canada had built a fleet but no one had developed the infrastructure on the coast to maintain it properly, let alone completely rebuild it.

The Atlantic Coast Command's most pressing demand in early 1942 was for the provision of modern radars to meet immediate operational needs and for improvements in habitability. In March a request for Staff policy on modernization was asked for, but the Naval Staff did not respond to repeated requests for support and guidance on the issue of modernization until the summer of 1942. At that time the Director of Naval Construction was cool to the idea of modernizing the first construction program ships, in large measure because of the complexity of the task, the inability of Canadian yards to cope with the work and the difficulty of obtaining the needed equipment from Britain. The rest of the Naval Staff lacked enthusiasm as well. Even the Director of Anti-Submarine Warfare (DA/SW) recommended caution. As the DA/SW pointed out, the new anti-submarine mortar, Hedgehog—the subject of modernization debates in 1942 and about which the Canadians then knew little—was due to be superseded by a better weapon.

Napanee, *undergoing modernization at Montreal in the summer of 1942. Her Type 271 radar had been fitted earlier—but that was the easy part, as her partially stripped-down bridge and forecastle suggest.*

The most the Director of Naval Construction was prepared to authorize in June 1942 were improvements which could be made with little effort. These included converting the Type 123A sonar to 123D by adding another standard magnetic compass binnacle and bearing indicator on the open bridge ahead of the sonar hut (so the captain did not have to duck inside during an action to get his bearings), and a loudspeaker system so the sonar operator could pass his information to those on the open bridge. These improvements had already been carried out on five of the British-owned ships, and were incorporated in the designs of the revised corvettes. Other simple improvements authorized by the end of the year included the construction of a housing just behind the bridge for the new 10-cm radar set, the Type 271, and the movement of the radar office from the former officers' toilet to the bridge. The fitting of Oerlikons on the bridge wings, and re-siting the mast astern of the bridge where it would not obstruct the forward search of the 271 radar, could also be done piecemeal.

Rather typically, the Naval Staff decided to wait to hear from the British before committing the navy to a wholesale program of modernization. An Admiralty anti-submarine mission, which visited Ottawa in early July following a trip to the USA, convinced the RCN of the need to modernize its corvettes. The Naval Staff then approved in principle the acquisition of the necessary gyros, plots, electric logs, low-power sets and other equipment needed to modernize the ships, including conversion of the Type 123A sonar to Type 144/145—the set needed to operate Hedgehog properly.[1] It was estimated that the program would take two years to complete and cost approximately two million dollars.

As an interim measure the Naval Staff further agreed on 20 August 1942 that corvette sonars should be immediately upgraded to Type 127DV, "to enable our corvettes to work in company with Admiralty corvettes." As a result, sonar—and modernization—policy got into something of a muddle. The Type 127DV was a radical improvement, as the staff knew, and a major step toward a complete Type 144/145 set. With the Type 127DV, the training of the sonar dome under the hull was done electronically (the Type 123 set was turned manually by a handwheel attached to a Bowden wire). The set required the addition of a large recorder and bearing plot, and because the oscillator itself was stabilized in azimuth (which held the sonar bearing regardless of the yawing of the ship), it also required a gyro compass. The RCN's Director of Naval Construction believed that it was possible to add the gyros and modernize the sonar without the addition of a low-power system. However, since the LP system would ultimately be needed for the firing control, night sight and illumination circuits of the Hedgehog, it was prudent to proceed with the installation of low power in conjunction with conversion of sonars to Type 127DV. There is no evidence in the Naval Staff minutes that the problem of rewiring before structural changes were made was seen as an issue.

The admission that Canadian corvettes, with their poor sonars and swinging magnetic compasses could not work in company with other escorts was a considerable indictment of the class and of the qualities of the escort fleet. The Naval Staff's endorsement of the modification of sonars from Type 123A to Type 127DV, as a piecemeal move towards modernization, suggests a poor understanding of the tasks ahead. The decision in August 1942 to move toward the Type 127DV sonar as an interim step to the latest Type 144/145 set also threw into question the earlier decision to upgrade the corvette's Type 123A set to 123D. Eventually, in early 1943 the staff rescinded its decision to proceed with Type 123D conversions, although the fitting of additional binnacles and loudspeakers was allowed.

The move to the Type 144/145 sonar, Hedgehog armament and gyro compass system promised a tremendous improvement in anti-submarine efficiency. The Hedgehog was a more accurate and efficient anti-submarine weapon than depth charges. Instead of running over the contact, losing it in the process and then pounding an area with high explosives in hopes of crushing the U-boat, the Hedgehog was a stand-off weapon. It allowed the escort to retain contact and its gyro-stabilization held the weapon on target in anything up to a 20-degree roll. The Hedgehog's twenty-four small "bombs," each carrying 32 pounds of Torpex, were fired forward of the ship to a range of 200 yards, where they fell in an oval 120 feet wide by 140 feet long. The bombs were contact fused, so explosions only occurred when the submarine or the bottom was hit, and were good to a depth of 1300 feet. The Hedgehog promised a much higher U-boat kill rate. The success rate in depth charge attacks during the war hovered around 6 percent, while Hedgehog success reached approximately 30 percent by 1944. Admiralty plans for installation of the Hedgehog called for a strengthening of the forecastle deck just ahead of the bridge, but in the Canadian short-forecastle corvettes that deck did not yet exist.

The Hedgehog was controlled by the Type 144/145 sonar (although it could be operated with the Type 127, but without complete electronic integration of the sonar and the weapon) and a gyro compass. The new system also required a complete rebuilding of the bridge, to carry a separate, new sonar hut with sufficient space for the sonar equipment, a plot, the anti-submarine officer and two operators. Sonar searches would now

---

1.   The Types 144 and 145 were basically the same set, except that the 145 had a portable dome. The RCN's ultimate objective was the Type 145 set, but many corvettes only got as far as fitting the Type 144.

*Rebuilding the bridge was central to modernization. Once the compass house was removed an open pilotage (centre), 20-mm Oerlikon mountings (left and right), and a new sonar hut (just forward of the pilotage) were built. This is a shot of **Brandon's** new bridge in November 1943.*

be controlled from the hut by the anti-submarine officer, who had to have good communications with the conning position—or pilotage—portion of the bridge. A gyro compass system was central to the new equipment and organization. In addition to its role in controlling the sonar set, gyro compass repeaters were to be fitted in the conning position, wheelhouse, captain's position on the bridge, sonar-directing gear compartment, and in the radar and direction-finding offices. Modernization was therefore a complex and lengthy task and some members of the Naval Staff, like the Director of Naval Construction, understood just how difficult it would be. Perhaps for that reason the march to modernization was a slow and piecemeal process in 1942.

One change decided upon in August could be readily carried out: the landing of the minesweeping gear still carried aboard the original corvettes. The need for this reserve minesweeping capability had passed with the commissioning of sufficient Bangor class minesweepers (themselves used largely as anti-submarine escorts) in early 1942. Corvettes also needed the extra space, especially for more depth charges (up to one hundred of which were now carried). Corvette captains were forced to retain a higher margin of fuel in their tanks as a reserve of ballast to compensate for rising top weight and this occurred at a time when operational authorities wanted increased endurance from their ships. Refuelling at sea, particularly for small ships, was still in its infancy in 1942, so low fuel still meant an early departure for port. The contract for removal of the sweep gear went to a Pictou, Nova Scotia, firm.

The modernized bridge from the forecastle, aboard **Edmundston** in Halifax, in the spring of 1943. The squat boxlike structure in the centre of the bridge is the sonar hut. The radar lantern behind it, designed for the Type 271, was at this time fitted with the new Canadian 10-cm set, the RXC, which proved to be a failure. Note the painting instructions chalked on the ship.

More extensive and important improvements, particularly the fitting of new weapons and radar, were hindered in late 1942 by basic administrative roadblocks. Canadian changes to the original corvette design, described in Chapter I, had led the RCN to restrict the adoption of some British improvements, such as heavier secondary weapons and even the breakwater on the forecastle, until stability trials could be conducted on Canadian ships. Therefore, alterations and additions authorized by the British for their corvettes had first to be authorized for Canadian escorts by the RCN "A&A" staff in Halifax. Newfoundland-based ships operating against the wolf packs in the mid-Atlantic in 1942, the ones most in need of modernization, routinely called at British ports where modifications could be done. However, MOEF ships could only obtain permission to undergo the modifications by first visiting Halifax. Implementation of piecemeal modernization in 1942 was therefore slow until the naval orders restricting alterations were amended. By the end of the year the RCN had given the Admiralty carte blanche to make improvements to RCN ships as opportunity presented itself, without the need of authorization from Canada.

In the meantime, orders for the equipment needed to modernize the ships were completed by the fall. However, the Naval Staff still lacked enthusiasm for modernization in late 1942. It was only at the end of the year that signals went out to east coast commands to report on the extent of fitting of modern equipment in the fleet, and the full details of the situation were not available to Ottawa until the spring of 1943. Moreover, the staff moved with caution once it decided in mid-1942 that modernization was essential. Work was authorized to begin on only one corvette, as a trial, in order to ascertain details of costs and time involved. This lead ship was to get the full treatment, but finding the time, place and resources to do even one ship proved insurmountable in 1942. The Staff had hoped to start with *Saskatoon* in August, but the navy, Halifax shipyards and the Department of Munitions and Supply apparently were unable to find the small amount of steel needed to complete the job, and the lead-ship project languished. *Sackville*, the next ship earmarked, went off to her regular scheduled refit in early January 1943 without going in for modernization. It was not until *Edmundston* was taken in hand by HM Dockyard, Halifax, on 4 January 1943 that the modernization program effectively commenced: six months after the Naval Staff had agreed on the need. The second corvette to begin modernization, *Calgary*, went into a yard at Cardiff, Wales, in early January as well. *Calgary* was chosen because she suffered from serious mechanical defects which required extensive dockyard repair, and it made sense to modernize her in the process. As a revised patrol vessel *Calgary* required little structural change: she was back in service by April.

What really gave impetus to modernization in 1943 was the crisis in the ocean escort groups at the end of 1942, discussed in Chapter III. Only in the wake of the transfer of Canadian escorts out of the mid-Atlantic in January was there a rapid refitting of the ships with the equipment to fight and win defensive battles against surfaced U-boats. Both corvettes and destroyers sported modern radar (Type 271) and heavier secondary armaments by the spring of 1943—thanks largely to direct Admiralty intervention. The British augmented Canadian groups with their own destroyers and frigates, and Canadian groups sailed with at least two HF/DF sets on hand. These were the improvements needed a year before, and had they been forthcoming, they would have markedly improved the performance of the fleet and in all likelihood kept it in the battle during the crucial months of early 1943.

Refitting the fleet for the "defensive" phase of the war, however, fell far short of full modernization. Spurred by the obvious shortcomings of the escorts, the Naval Staff finally decided in February 1943 to press ahead with the complete set of modifications in all the

corvettes before waiting details of *Edmundston*'s conversion. As had been anticipated, this was easier said than done. When asked about the prospects of refitting the fleet quickly in 1943, the Supervising Naval Engineer, Maritimes, in Halifax was pessimistic. As the SNEM reported, new construction, including merchant ships, had priority over refits in Canadian yards; the work force available to handle the work was too small, and in any event, capacity on the east coast was inadequate. The chief engineer in Newfoundland, when asked about the prospects for the refitting schedule, complained that the idea of losing ships from operations for ten weeks was appalling: in the event he would lose his ships for much longer than that.

Officers in Halifax estimated that perhaps half of the fleet might be modernized in Canadian yards during 1943, an estimate the Chief of Naval Engineering and Construction rightly considered optimistic. Maritime yards were small, undermanned, lacked experience in major work, lacked the clout to obtain supplies; they suffered from indifferent management and in some cases from strained labour-management relations. Skilled younger tradesmen had either been called up for army service or were working under deferrals which promised a call to arms in the near future. The remainder of the work force was either inexperienced or old.

Indeed, it seems that many of the east coast yards did not understand, when approached in early 1943 about modernization, that this was more than an annual refit. Refits themselves often took three to four months to complete in Atlantic Canada in early 1943. With the exception of Halifax—already taxed to the limit—there seems to have been no one place where all the necessary work could be done simultaneously. *Sackville* went to refit in Liverpool, NS, in mid-January and stayed alongside at Thompson Brothers until late March. She then sailed to Halifax for docking and on to Pictou to have her minesweeping gear removed. Work-ups followed and the corvette returned to operations in early May. Her refit lasted about twenty weeks, and she still had a short forecastle, outdated bridge and none of the modern navigation and sonar equipment needed.

By the spring of 1943 modernization was moving, but slowly. While virtually all RCN corvettes carried or were being fitted with 10-cm radar, by mid-June only *Edmundston* had had her forecastle extended (apart from the remaining British corvettes on loan and, of course the revised corvettes), although a further ten short-forecastle corvettes were in process of extension. *Calgary*, *Edmundston*, *Snowberry*, and *Trillium* had Hedgehog and thirteen more were fitting. Thus, only two out of approximately seventy RCN corvettes had been modernized by June 1943. Figures from the RN for later in the summer (received by the RCN in August) revealed the backwardness of the Canadian fleet: of the sixty British corvettes in Western Approaches Command at the time, only two were believed to have neither extended forecastles nor Hedgehog. Of the fifty-eight partially modernized ships, forty-three had Hedgehog and nine were in process of fitting it. As explained below, by mid-1943 this dearth of modern equipment in the Canadian corvette fleet again affected the tasks to which they were assigned.

The bottleneck on the east coast offered no easy solutions, so the RCN sought help from abroad. The Admiralty relieved some of the pressure by arranging to have its eight remaining corvettes on loan to the RCN fully modernized in the US under lend-lease. The British also promised to attempt to find spaces in UK yards to modernize a further six RCN corvettes in 1943. That still left the RCN with a large shortfall—about fifty ships—even assuming that east coast yards could do the work expected.

Problems in equipment supply plagued both planning and actual work in early 1943. As the program got underway in earnest in June, it was discovered that electrical equipment needed for modernization was in short supply, and this despite the fact that the detailed requirements had been worked out the previous October. Evidently, the preliminary contract demand did not go to the Department of Munitions and Supply until February 1943, and since it was not marked "urgent," it had not been acted upon until April. In this instance the navy was saved—as it would be many years later in the Gulf War—by being able to draw on equipment already on order for new construction.

Squeezing the ships into existing dockyard space in 1943 was not easy. The British did only three more for the RCN after *Calgary*, and Canadian yards took an inordinately long time to complete the ships they took over in 1943. While British yards, when pushed, modernized corvettes (extended forecastle and improved bridge) in an average of fifteen weeks and US yards turned the RCN's corvettes around in about ten, corvettes sent to Canadian yards in 1943 languished for an average of twenty-two weeks. In the end, only

eighteen corvettes were modernized in Canadian yards during 1943, and the pace was slow: *New Westminster*, modernized at Sydney Foundry and Machine Company, took seven months. A fair portion of this time seems to have been spent lying alongside at Halifax as the naval dockyard redid some of the work completed by the smaller yards. The RCN also sought further assistance in the US during 1943. In addition to the RCN-manned British corvettes refitted under lend-lease, by the end of the year *Collingwood*, *Dunvegan*, *Agassiz*, *Drumheller*, *Oakville*, and *Wetaskiwin* had gone south. In all, five corvettes completed modernization in American yards during 1943, bringing the total for the year up to twenty-six: less than half and well short of the optimistic projections at the start of the year.

In fairness to the hard-pressed and inexperienced east coast yards, delays there appear to have been exacerbated by difficulties in obtaining much of the vital equipment from Britain and the US. Shortages of both brass and electrical fittings made it all but impossible to establish firm completion dates, and as early as mid-1943 the Staff at Halifax considered not attempting any more modernizations until those in hand were completed. Shortages of the latest sonars for corvettes, the Type 144 with a fixed dome, became a particular bottleneck by the end of the year. The RCN was forced to settle for the Type 127D as an interim measure until the Type 144/145 sets were available in numbers (as they were from Canadian sources by early 1944). Ironically, most of the Type 144 sets went to the new Increased Endurance corvettes of the 1942-1943 and 1943-1944 programs (discussed in the next chapter). The result was that, with the final upgrade of sonars from Type 127D to 145, the corvettes of the first construction programs—as a group—had better sonars at the end of the war than did those corvettes which commissioned in 1944.

The difficulties encountered in 1943, coupled with the favourable developments in the course of the war and the appearance of many newer and better classes of escorts, led the Naval Staff to consider abandoning the modernization of the remaining short-forecastle corvettes in December 1943. In the end, for reasons of morale aboard those ships, it was agreed that improvements were necessary. During 1944, fifteen completed modernizations in US yards, one in UK and twenty-three in Canadian yards. Ultimately, twelve RCN corvettes were never modernized. Apart from those lost, these included *Chicoutimi*, *Nanaimo*, *Rosthern*, *The*

The increasing sophistication of sonars is well illustrated by this Type 127DV control equipment in the sonar hut of **Rimouski** *in November 1943: compare it to the photo of the Type 123A in Chapter I.*

Pas, and *Brantford*, all of which ended the war with short forecastles, original bridges with all the ad hoc improvements and Type 123 sonars. These unmodernized ships did, however, receive many other improvements, such as Type 271 radar, upgraded secondary armament (but no Hedgehog) and had their masts re-sited aft of the wheelhouse.

The objective of modernization was a ship designed for ocean escort duties, with vastly improved accommodation, a warship's bridge with the latest in navigational aids, modern electronics (including radar and sonar, as well as radio), and better weapons. Although not all modernized corvettes emerged the same, in terms of weaponry the ideal at the end of 1943 was as follows:

    1   4" QF Mk.XIX main gun
    2   20-mm Oerlikons on the bridge
    1   2-pdr in the gun tub aft
    4   additional 20-mm positions prepared (usually
        on the engine room casing)

1 complete Hedgehog mounting
72 depth charges.

The RCN had also hoped to fit Mk. IV depth charge throwers, which the British included in their corvette modernization. The Mk.II depth charge thrower, which all Canadian corvettes (except Castles) carried, hurled both the carrier (or cradle) and depth charge in the firing process. The Mk.IV retained the cradle, making the reloading process a one-step procedure—putting the next depth charge in place. In the end the RCN had to reserve the Mk.IV thrower for frigates, and its corvette crews had to load both cradle and charge to the end of the war.

Modernization also involved an enormous change in the electronics fitted to the ships. By 1944 all corvettes had been fitted with the Type 271 10-cm surface warning radar, either in the original form with a "bird-cage" type housing or the later variant with a clear, one-piece "Perspex" housing. They retained their earlier type SW2C at the masthead as an air warning set,

*Hedgehog—the weapon of choice in the modernization battle. This fitting is aboard **Moose Jaw** in 1944; it could be adjusted to point fifteen degrees either side of the bow. The bombs here have their safety caps (removed before firing) over the arming propellers.*

although with a new X-shaped antenna. The ships also carried IFF (Interrogation Friend or Foe, for aircraft identification) antennas, as well as those for wireless and radio telephones. A simple comparison of as-completed photographs from 1941 with a late-war shot reveals how sophisticated the corvette had become.

Escort modernization proved to be the single biggest problem faced by the RCN during 1943, and its repercussions were felt throughout the navy. By the middle of the year the failure to equip the ships with the latest weapons and sensors began seriously to affect morale as well as operational tasking. As the war moved into its offensive stage, the lack of modern radar, sonars and anti-submarine weapons meant that RCN escorts, which were now able to defend convoys adequately, were increasingly relegated to defensive roles while active prosecution of U-boat contacts was assigned to better-equipped RN ships.

Although the senior officers of the fleet were more or less aware of this problem, and had some sense of the discontent it fomented, the issue was forced to a boil in August 1943. In that month Capt W. Strange, the Assistant Director of Naval Intelligence, took passage to Britain in the British destroyer *Duncan*, whose commander complained that Canada's excellent effort at sea was being crippled by the lack of modern equipment on its ships. Strange was vaguely aware of the situation from his discussions with Canadian officers, and was persuaded to prepare a confidential memorandum for Naval Minister Angus L. Macdonald. At the same time Cdr K. F. Adams, who had recently gone back to sea as captain of the destroyer *Assiniboine*, sent a similar memo to Naval Headquarters through proper channels.

Both Strange's and Adams' memos concentrated on equipment on the corvettes. Strange noted that, as of August, only five RN corvettes were *without* gyro-compasses and Hedgehog, both key to effective anti-submarine warfare by mid-1943, while only two RCN corvettes (presumably *Edmundston* and *Calgary*) had so far been fitted. This lack of modern equipment, Strange claimed with justification, "prevented our ships from making a good showing" and relegated them to secondary tasks. Adams echoed the sentiment in his memo.

*In addition to new electronics and anti-submarine weapons, modernization also meant that most corvettes finally got the 2-pdr pom-pom gun their after gun position was designed for, like this one on **Sorel** in early 1944.*

*Depth charges remained a vital weapon in the corvette's inventory until the end of the war—if anything, they tended to carry more. **Edmundston's** quarterdeck during modernization in 1943 already has the minesweeping winch replaced by extra depth charge storage (foreground), and her minesweeping davits have been replaced by a small, removable one in a central position for reloading the rails. The markings on the depth charges, actually a green diamondlike pattern and a red stripe, indicate they are filled with amatol. The bars arching over her quarterdeck were to support a towing wire, which attached to the engine room casing directly above the rudder post.*

What it all looked like put together: **Orillia** *in her fully modernized form, 9 August 1944.*

The Naval Minister, Angus L. Macdonald, was sensitive to the performance of the fleet in the late summer of 1942 because the federal government was desperately seeking some means of shaking Canadians from their war-weariness and anti-government mood. The Canadian army had yet to enter the fighting in a major way: its despatch to Sicily in July 1943 was designed to get it fighting and was the result of considerable Canadian pressure. The RCAF overseas, locked in a grim bombing campaign, offered little that Canadians could relate to. The government would clearly have prospered from some positive news of Canadian naval victories against U-boats: convoys successfully escorted was not enough. In the slow march of corvette modernization, Macdonald eventually became convinced he had found a major flaw in the administration of the navy, and that the RCN had let down its men, the Canadian people and the federal government. After a long and bitter exchange of correspondence between himself and the Chief of the Naval Staff, P. W. Nelles, over responsibility for the failure to modernize ships sooner, Macdonald finally fired Nelles at the end of 1943. It was an incident which reflected badly on both men, and ended with Canada's single most important Chief of Naval Staff retiring a bitter and resentful man.

CHAPTER V

New Types And Late-War Operations, 1943-1945

The appearance of new war-built classes of anti-submarine and escort vessels—River, Loch and Colony Class frigates, and destroyer escorts—in considerable numbers during 1943 finally removed corvettes from the centre stage of the war at sea. Much of the direct contact with the enemy now fell to powerful hunting and support groups of more capable ships. Indeed, by the last year and a half of the war, only the RCN used corvettes in what might be called first-line escort duty. The reasons for this were twofold. First, the RCN continued to build and acquire advanced types of corvettes after the RN had switched its acquisition programs to newer classes of escorts. Second, RCN escort responsibilities in the North Atlantic continued to expand following the defeat of the wolf packs in 1943, so large numbers of escorts were still needed. However, the reduction in German activity and the advent of trans-Atlantic air patrols permitted less than state-of-the-art types to escort oceanic convoys safely.

The year 1943 was the last in which corvettes carried a disproportionate share of the fighting, and Canadian ships did their part. The Torch corvettes had a particularly hectic period in the first months of the year, with their normal routine of escorting support convoys from Britain to North Africa interrupted by submarine sinkings and lost ships. *Ville de Québec* started the action on the afternoon of 13 January, ninety miles west of Algiers. She gained an underwater contact and dropped one pattern of charges on it. As the corvette opened the distance to renew the sonar search *U 224* rose bow first to the surface. *Ville de Québec*'s gunners opened fire while the corvette spun around and set course to ram. The escort's bow struck *U 224* hard between the conning tower and the forward gun, rending the pressure hull and sending the U-boat to the bottom in four minutes. The whole affair, as the RCN's official history observed, "from contact to kill, had taken just ten minutes."

Six days later *Port Arthur*, another revised corvette, located the Italian submarine *Tritone* by sonar as it closed the corvette's convoy. *Tritone* was new, and was experiencing serious problems maintaining her trim when submerged. *Port Arthur*'s first depth charge pattern drove the submarine down to four hundred feet, smashing fittings inside the sub and forcing the Italians into a decision to surface. When they did so they were met by a hail of fire from the British destroyer *Antelope*, which also prevented *Port Arthur* from ramming.

*The corvette in its final form: **Owen Sound** at Collingwood, November 1943. She shows the characteristics of the modified corvettes: the raised main gun platform with its new Mk.XIX gun, the raised bridge, whaler on the starboard side, absence of boiler-room ventilators and sleek hull lines.*

*A closer look at the forward portion of the late-war corvettes, in this case the British-built **Long Branch** alongside at Halifax in November 1944. Like the other three modified corvettes obtained from the British, she retains the older, Mk.IX main gun.*

Smiths Falls *about to receive her water-tube boilers, Kingston, Ontario, August 1944: compare this with the shot of boilers going aboard Galt in Chapter I.*

Eventually, *Tritone*'s crew surrendered and the riddled submarine sank.

On 8 February it was *Regina*'s turn. She gained contact with the Italian submarine *Avorio* at night by radar, tracking its movements until the submarine dived. *Regina* made one depth charge attack and then waited ten minutes to see what would happen. As she moved in to attack again, the white wake of a surfaced submarine appeared and the corvette opened fire with the bridge Oerlikons. Tracers from these were used to direct the 4-inch gun, which eventually struck the submarine at the base of the conning tower. At that point return fire from *Avorio* ceased and the crew poured onto the deck, making signs of surrender. *Regina*'s attempt at salvage was frustrated by the gaping hole where the 4-inch shell hit, and after about a half hour *Avorio* sank.

Three submarines in less than a month was a remarkable feat for Canada's corvette fleet. They were aided by the heavier secondary armament and modern radar that came with the Torch operation, the additional training available at British bases, more favourable sea conditions in the Mediterranean and some inept ship handling on the part of their opponents. Two other kills were recorded by Canadian corvettes supporting the North African campaign in early 1943. On 4 March, group C-1, on one of its Mediterranean runs while undergoing re-equipment and training in the UK, fought a battle around MKS.10. In the process *Shediac* gained contact with *U 87*, which was actually in transit through the area. With assistance from others in the group *Shediac* destroyed the sub.

Shediac's victory was accredited shortly after the war, in the initial Allied re-evaluations of German losses. Further re-evaluation of all U-boat kills conducted in the late 1980s credited another Torch corvette, *Prescott*, with the destruction of *U 163* on 13 March in the eastern Atlantic. *Prescott* was escorting MKS.9, a slow Gibraltar-to-UK convoy, when she got a radar contact on a U-boat that soon dived. As *Prescott* raced in to deliver her depth charge attack, she sighted a second apparent U-boat on the surface in the direction of the convoy. She

Fergus, the last corvette to commission into the RCN, at Collingwood in late 1944. The modified corvettes retained the flattened stern, originally designed to carry minesweeping gear, but the depth charge chutes were closer together and aligned parallel.

delivered a five-charge pattern on the submerged target and then turned away to track the second. It too dived and *Prescott* delivered a nine-charge pattern. *Napanee* then joined for a deliberate search during which *Prescott* attacked one dubious contact. It was all very inconclusive at the time, but postwar analysis revealed that *U 163* was the only U-boat in the area at the time, and *Prescott*'s attacks were the only ones which can account for her disappearance.

In all, Canadian corvettes supporting Torch accounted for five enemy submarines: a very commendable record. But the battle was by no means one-sided. On 6 February *Louisburg* was sunk by an aerial torpedo from an Italian aircraft during an attack on convoy KMS.8 off the Algerian coast: the only Canadian corvette sunk by air attack. The torpedo struck *Louisburg*'s engine room, killing most of the watch on duty there. The rest of the crew abandoned ship smoothly, including one officer who went over the side in a coonskin coat, prompting a comment from the darkness, "Joe College goes to sea!" Whatever levity there was soon ended as *Louisburg* plummetted to the bottom and depth charges exploded, killing and wounding men in the water. In all, thirty-eight officers and men perished.

The heavy casualties from *Louisburg*'s depth charge explosions prompted the RCN to alter the boat and Carley float allocation to Canadian corvettes. In order to ensure that men would be clear of the water, the Naval Staff in early April 1943 decided to replace the two 16-foot rowboats carried either side of the corvette's funnel with a single 27-foot whaler (usually carried on the starboard side) and enough Carley floats for 150 percent of crew strength.

Exploding depth charges also dramatically increased the casualties in the other corvette lost in the Torch operations, *Weyburn*. She struck a mine just west of Gibraltar on 22 February shortly after joining a convoy. The explosion ripped open the portside amidships, splitting the funnel from bottom to top, buckling the deck, letting the sea into the engine room and causing pipes to burst. Although the corvette settled deep in the water, the boiler rooms and forward portion of the ship remained tight. Primers for all depth charges except two, which were jammed by the explosion, were removed and salvage operations begun. The British destroyer *Wivern* arrived and, nudging her bow against the stricken corvette's stern, began to take off *Weyburn*'s crew. About twenty minutes

later something—probably a bulkhead—in *Weyburn* gave way, her bow rose sharply in the air and in a few seconds she was gone. Three men on the bridge and several still in the water died instantly when the two depth charges with the jammed primers exploded. *Wivern* was badly damaged and crewmen from both ships in the destroyer's forward sections were seriously injured.

The success of Canadian corvettes in distant waters—including *Oakville*'s in the Caribbean—suggested that, given a chance, RCN escorts were good at destroying submarines. The problem in the mid-ocean in late 1942 had been their inability to *defend* convoys. Unfortunately, corvettes operating from Canadian bases lacked access to either the necessary equipment, training and even concentrations of enemy action to produce comparable results. Home-based corvettes were, in 1942-1943, typically the most behind in fitting new equipment, and by the spring of 1943 this had begun to affect their tactical employment. New tactics recommended for Western Local Escort Forces in 1943, for example, reflect the weakness of Halifax-based corvettes.

The threat in inshore waters was always from solitary U-boats attacking targets of opportunity. Whereas MOEF escorts could expect to deal with a pack of U-boats and had to concentrate on maintaining a fighting defence of their convoys, WLEF sailors knew that should a ship be torpedoed, the convoy could be left unescorted without fear of further immediate attacks. This left WLEF free to pursue solitary attackers, and new tactics developed in early 1943 were designed to make the most of the particular strengths of each WLEF escort type to find and destroy the U-boat. Ships with the best radars, typically destroyers, and sonars—destroyers and Bangors—were placed on the likely approach routes, and these vessels were given active search roles in the wake of an attack. The Bangor Class minesweeper was tasked to conduct a careful triangular search for the U-boat around the stricken vessel, while the group's destroyer made a wider sweep of the whole vicinity with its 10-cm radar. The corvette in the group was relegated to rescue and salvage work. It was a sad irony. The RCN's principal anti-submarine escort vessel, which began life as an auxiliary minesweeper, did the menial rescue and salvage work, while the fleet's principal minesweeper did the anti-submarine search.

The weaknesses in WLEF did not last long. During the spring of 1943 Canadian corvettes on loan to the

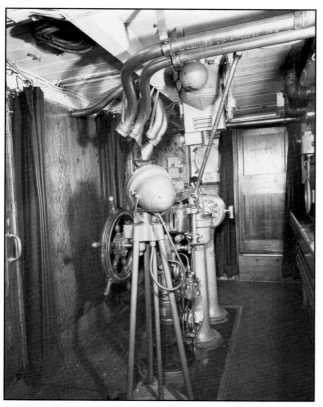

*The spartan wheelhouse of the modified corvette **Atholl.***

British from the mid-ocean and for Torch and the Americans for southern US and Caribbean waters were returned to Canada as the RCN endeavoured to consolidate. This was part and parcel of modernization efforts, and it gave the Canadian fleet a much better balance of forces through its areas of responsibility. It also permitted the RCN to move more aggressively into the offensive phase of the war—to take the war to the enemy in the manner of American hunter-killer and British support groups. The improved and modernized corvettes allowed this to happen, albeit with mixed results, in mid-1943.

Nevertheless, the Canadian move into offensive operations against U-boats, as part of the general Allied trend by mid-1943, was still hindered by an overall shortage of modernized corvettes and more capable ships, like frigates or destroyers. This affected the RCN in two ways. First, it meant that any U-boat contacts made by Canadian close escort groups were passed to the closest British ships to prosecute. It was this sad fact that propelled the modernization issue into a full-blown crisis by August. Canadian sailors were tired

of playing second fiddle to their British counterparts and wanted their ships modernized. Messages were sent direct to the Minister of the Naval Service by officers, ignoring official channels, and accusing the Naval Staff of bungling incompetence. Canadian sailors wanted to know why only two of their fleet of seventy corvettes had been modernized when only two of the sixty British corvettes in Western Approaches Command had *not* been. The government, under considerable pressure politically from a war-weary electorate, wanted U-boat kills in order to make headlines: good defensive convoy escort work was not enough. In the end, heads rolled at Naval Service Headquarters, including that of the Chief of the Naval Staff.

But the Naval Staff was as anxious as anyone to keep the RCN in the thick of the fight. The problem in mid-1943 was how to do it with a largely corvette fleet. Both the British and the Americans were charging about the Atlantic sinking submarines with groups of modern, well-equipped, long-range frigates, destroyers, destroyer escorts and small aircraft carriers. The RCN's solution was groups of mixed escort types, with numbers—as usual—made up by corvettes. These groups came under the operational control of the British Commander-in-Chief Western Approaches, who used them either to reinforce the escort of threatened convoys or to search promising areas where intelligence suggested U-boats might be lurking. The second Canadian support group to be established, EG-9, made history in the battle for convoys ONS.18/ON.202 in September 1943. That combined convoy was the first to be attacked by German acoustic homing torpedoes, as the U-boats attempted to blast their way through the escort screen to get at the ships. EG-9's core, the Canadian destroyer *St Croix* and the British frigate *Itchen*, were sunk by acoustic torpedoes, and the group's corvettes, *Chambly, Morden* and *Sackville*, had acoustic torpedoes detonated in their wakes. The loss of EG-9's two stalwarts led to the temporary disbandment of the group.

However, by the end of 1943 there were three Canadian support groups operating in the mid-Atlantic; EG-6, a reformed EG-9 and C-2 (temporarily released from close-escort duty). Each of these groups contained

*A wealth of detail is revealed in this marvellous study of the stern of two of the modified class: **Louisburg (II)** on the left and an unidentified corvette, possibly **Lindsay** (note the 20-mm mounting well aft).* ➤

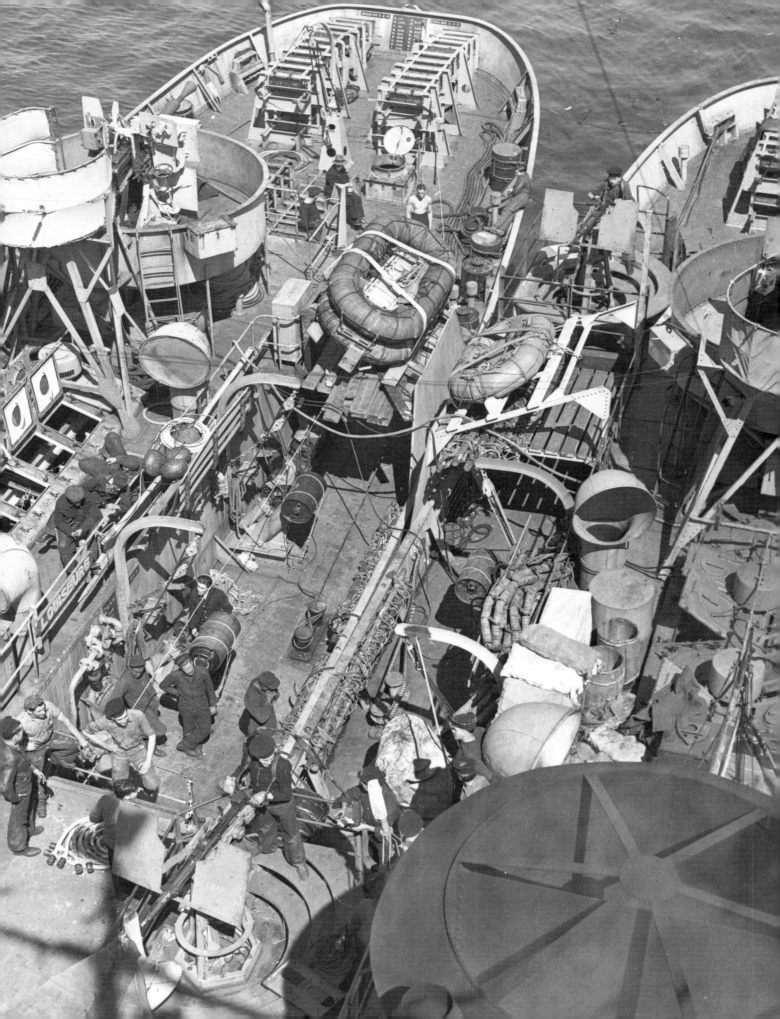

a few corvettes. They could not keep pace with the destroyers and frigates of their groups, and in practice the groups tended to operate in two divisions, with the corvettes forming one part. Despite their limited range, the corvettes did excellent work and contributed to the destruction of three U-boats over the winter of 1943-1944. In late November *Snowberry* and *Calgary* of EG-6, operating in support of a convoy, found and sank *U 536*, and in early January 1944 *Camrose* shared the destruction of *U 757* with HMS *Bayntun*. C-2 got its chance in March in a marathon hunt for *U 744*, which ended after thirty-two hours and the expenditure of 291 depth charges, totalling 87,300 pounds of high explosive; *Chilliwack* and *Fennel* shared the victory with five other ships.

These contributions to the Allied destruction of U-boats by the veterans of the early building programs were something of a swan song for corvettes in the front line of the anti-submarine war. Support groups needed to stay at sea as long as possible, cover wide distances, move quickly and carry the very latest in weaponry. The early corvettes which contributed to the support group operations over the winter of 1943-1944 were a stopgap until the frigates arrived. When they did, the corvette retreated to the essential but more mundane tasks of close escort, and there they remained for the balance of the war.

By late 1943 and early 1944 corvette ranks were also being filled by a new generation of the class, a generation which had the range, seakeeping and equipment to do the task first asked of corvettes in 1941. Not surprisingly then, the origins of the final Canadian corvette programs of 1942-1943 and 1943-1944 can be traced to early 1942. With most of the 1939-1940 programs all but completed, and Canadian yards in need of work and under pressure from the rapidly expanding war, the Canadian Naval Staff had to decide in early 1942 what classes of escorts and what numbers to build. Clearly there was now a requirement for a mid-ocean anti-submarine escort, something not part of the earlier programs, and corvettes were considered unsuited for that task. The focus of building for ocean escort was to rest with the new Twin-Screw Corvettes. This was a new design built around two corvette power plants, 100 feet more hull to ride the ocean swell, 7,200-mile range—more than twice that of the first corvettes—3 knots faster (at 19), better accommodation and much heavier weaponry. The British already had ships of this type on order from

Canadian yards in early 1942 and the RCN saw in them the answer to its trans-Atlantic escort needs. Twin-Screw Corvettes was an awkward name for the new escort class, so the Chief of the Canadian Naval Staff, Adm Percy Nelles, dubbed them "frigates," and with that a long-abandoned classification for naval vessels reappeared in the naval lexicon. All but three of the seventy frigates operated by the RCN by the end of the war were River class (following the British decision to name their own after rivers), although in Canadian service most carried the names of cities and towns.

Placing orders for frigates for the RCN in Canadian yards was delayed in 1942 as supplies and suitable dockyards were sorted out. In the meantime, the staff ordered a new batch of corvettes—sixteen in all. As Gilbert Tucker, the official naval historian, relates, these corvettes were "intended primarily for escorting coastal convoys." Although the Naval Minister objected to the construction of more "obsolete" ships, it was unthinkable to have Canadian yards standing idle while the outcome of the war was being decided. As corvettes went, the 1942-1943 program was anything but obsolete. All of the lessons of wartime experience were pulled together into what came to be known as Increased Endurance Corvettes. The improved sheer and flare of the revised corvette hull formed the basis of the new ships, but what sets them apart externally from the earlier revised corvettes was their superstructure. The bridge of these late-war corvettes was a full deck higher and built from the outset to naval standards. The platform for the 4-inch gun was also raised, to clear spray and provide a better field of fire, and it was connected directly to the wheelhouse level of the bridge by a wide platform. This gave the modified ships a quite distinctive and powerful appearance.

The larger platform not only eased access to the gun, and provided the ready crews with shelter in poor weather, but the new ahead-throwing anti-submarine weapon Hedgehog was mounted there as well. A new 4-inch gun was also ordered for these ships, the quick-firing Mk.XIX. The gun was semi-automatic and, unlike the old main gun of the earlier corvettes, used fixed ammunition (shell and brass propellant casing fixed together like a huge rifle round). The new ammunition and firing system, coupled with an ability to elevate the gun to 60 degrees, gave the Mk.XIX gun an anti-aircraft capability and a much more rapid rate of fire.

Another distinguishing feature of this corvette type was its upright funnel, and the absence of the hooded boiler room ventilators around the funnel itself. The straight funnel was designed to prevent submarines from determining, at a distance or under poor light, just how the ship lay. The missing ventilators were evidence of further improvements to the boiler system. Modified corvettes adopted a "forced draught," closed boiler room, in which the air pressure was maintained at a higher pressure by fans mounted on the funnel casing. These fans eliminated the need for the large, hooded ventilators that characterized earlier types of corvettes. In fact, the modernization of the RPVs of the 1940-1941 program made them virtually indistinguishable from the IE except for the tell-tale presence of the ventilators around the funnel.

What the photographs do not reveal is one of the most important improvements in the late-war corvettes: increased endurance. By augmenting the fuel storage in the design, the IEs doubled the range of the original design to 7400 nautical miles at 10 knots. This and the hull improvements made these corvettes very good ocean escorts, and that is how the RCN eventually used them.

The decision to order sixteen IE corvettes from Canadian yards in early 1942 was followed by a review of shipbuilding capacity, prompted in good measure by the desire to find a way to build as many frigates as possible. The review revealed two basic things: Canada had more capacity—overall—than anticipated, but frigates could not be built in the Great Lakes yards because they were too long to pass through the then existing locks on the St Lawrence River. Concentrating frigate construction in yards outside the Great Lakes left surplus capacity in Ontario, where only small ships could be built. The RCN preferred to concentrate on the new Algerine class minesweeper, a design that incorporated two engines (compared to the corvette's one). However, switching some yards engaged in corvette production to Algerines promised lengthy delays and so to avoid that, to keep these yards busy and get ships to sea, a small program of IE corvettes—twelve ships—was ordered from the Great Lakes as the 1943-1944 program. Thus the final decisions about corvette acquisition were dictated more by the limitations of Great Lakes yards and St Lawrence locks than by the assessed needs of the navy.

Ontario yards not dependent upon repeat corvette orders were switched to Algerines, which the RCN planned to compete as escorts. The Algerines' shallow draught made them poor anti-submarine ships, prone to rolling, and the hull configuration was not conducive to a comfortable ride. When the British learned that Canadian Algerines were to be built for escort duty they offered to trade corvettes for them. The offer included four of the ten IE corvettes then building in UK yards, and twelve of a radically new kind of corvette, the Castle class. The RCN accepted. The four UK-built IE corvettes entered Canadian service in the winter of 1943-1944, and were among the first to do so. They can be easily distinguished from their Canadian counterparts by the short mainmast on the engine room casing, which normally carried the ensign. The British offer to trade IE corvettes for Algerines meant that the RCN became the principal operator of this type of corvette: of the fifty-two built, thirty-one served in the Canadian navy.

The Castle class were altogether different. They represent the pursuit of the basic corvette to its ultimate form and its adaption to ocean-escort duty. They are, in fairness, a separate class unto themselves, but since they were technically corvettes they are included here for completeness.

The addition of nearly fifty feet to the hull reduced much of the cramping of the original corvette designs. The length, while not enough to straddle the Atlantic wave interval, allowed the ship to ride ocean swells comfortably. Good seakeeping and a good draught made for a good anti-submarine platform, and these were from the outset anti-submarine warships. The weapons suit was significantly different from that of any other corvette, in that Castles were designed to take the second generation of ahead-throwing anti-submarine mortar, Squid. This three-tube launcher was mounted on the superstructure just behind the main gun. The Castle class's single Squid mounting fired three very heavy, hydrostatically detonated bombs well ahead of the ship. Like depth charges, the triangular Squid pattern was designed to produce a three-dimensional explosion which crushed the U-boat's pressure hull. The Squid itself was slaved to a new sonar, the Type 147B, which could read both depth and range. Targeting data was passed automatically to the bombs by the sonar, including depth settings, and the firing sequence was controlled by the sonar. Like Hedgehog, Squid allowed the ships to stand off from the target and keep it in sonar contact while the attack took place. But Squid's automation, its superb sonar control and the power of the bombs made it a far more lethal weapon than Hedgehog—and sailors got a satisfying "bang" each time.

Squid was the most successful anti-submarine weapon of the war, by 1945 achieving a kill rate of 50 percent. One RCN Castle class corvette, *St Thomas*, destroyed *U 877* on 27 December 1944, the only Canadian victory by a Squid during the war. According to *St Thomas*'s captain, L. P. Denny, he only ever fired two Squid bombs in anger: the first fired manually to keep *U 877* down and the second—a single shot—fired by the corvette's anti-submarine system as she slowly advanced over the U-boat. "It was," Denny recalled, "as easy as duck soup." Because of their superior capabilities, some British Castle class corvettes were formed into offensive anti-submarine support groups by 1945. For reasons still unknown, the RCN kept this lethal weapon tied to its trans-Atlantic escort groups while the active pursuit of enemy submarines was conducted by its frigates with their much less effective Hedgehogs.

Castle class ships were also distinguished by the large, naval standard bridge, the lattice mast surmounted by the ultimate in British wartime surface escort radar, and by the virtual emptiness of their quarterdecks. The bridge, and in fact the whole command and control arrangement of the ship, was designed to naval specifications, including the extensive internal communications system. The masthead radar, the Type 272, was a 10-cm set with much greater power than the standard Type 271 of most escorts. The added height and power gave 272-equipped ships an enormous advantage. Some RCN Castles were fitted with the even more powerful and effective Type 277 radar.

Castles also carried a gun armament capable of handling any surfaced U-boat and most air threats. Its main gun was the same as that authorized for the IEs, the Mk.XIX quick-firer on a high-angle/low-angle mount. Single 20-mm Oerlikons were mounted on the bridge wings and two twin 20-mm powered Oerlikon mountings were carried in raised positions aft. What Castles did not have a lot of was depth charges. While most wartime escorts stacked depth charges in great heaps, the Castle class carried only one rail and two throwers with a total of fifteen charges. With the Squid they had little need of the old system.

Castle class corvettes were the most handsome and the best equipped of anti-submarine vessels in the Atlantic war. The RCN's reasons for acquiring them, however, seem to have nothing to do with aesthetics or modern weaponry. The RCN weapon of choice in the anti-submarine war in 1942 and 1943 was the Hedgehog, and the Naval Staff remained decidedly cool toward Squid throughout 1944. The acquisition of the Castles appears to have been a case of the British offering and the RCN accepting.

Orders for Castles were also placed in Canadian yards in 1943, but the general resolution of the U-boat problem in 1943 led to the cancellation of major building programs and these were never laid down. All forty-four Castle class ships were completed in British yards, five of them as rescue ships. Twenty-six served with the RN, one went to the Norwegians and the remaining twelve to the RCN. Their use as close escorts of trans-Atlantic convoys during the last eight months of the war seems a waste of a powerful resource, although on occasion Canadian Castles were used for area searches in British waters.

These new corvettes—the 1942-1943, 1943-1944 IE programs, the IEs acquired from Britain and the Castle class ships—formed the backbone of the mid-ocean groups during the last eighteen months of the war. They faced a radically different kind of war in 1944-1945 from that which had tested the earlier corvettes. By early 1944 the main convoy routes in the Atlantic had become something of a milk run. Oppressive Allied airpower and the relentless pursuit by support and hunter-killer groups made life precarious for German submariners and pretty humdrum for the close escorts of convoys. Nonetheless, the possibility of a major German offensive against the main trade convoys remained until the end of the war. In fact, a large wolf pack operation was mounted against trans-Atlantic convoys in early 1945: it was virtually annihilated by American hunter-killer groups. It was prudent therefore for the RCN to maintain a strong and modern force in defence of these convoys.

While the new corvettes carried the burden of ocean escort, the older corvettes actually saw most of the action. Allied airpower forced submarines inshore by early 1944, into the zones where the older ships operated, while at the same time Canadian corvettes were assigned hazardous tasks in European coastal waters. The genesis of this somewhat ironic development—with the latest ships going to the quiet theatre while the old ships saw the action—has to do in large part with Operation Neptune: the invasion of France in June 1944. The RN withdrew all its forces from

One of the key improvements that came with the Mk.XIX gun was fixed ammunition, seen here being used in gun drill aboard **Louisburg (II)** late in the war.

Castle class corvettes were the most handsome of all war-built escorts, with fine lines and a nicely balanced superstructure. They were also among the best anti-submarine ships of the war. Unfortunately **Leaside**, seen here in June 1945, was one of only twelve in RCN service.

*The business end of a Castle class, in this case **Huntsville** at Halifax in November 1944. The shrouded weapon on the small deck ahead of the bridge is a single Squid mounting, the tracks for its loading trolley visible to the right. Single 20-mm Oerlikons are on either side of the bridge and a Mk.XIX gun is forward.*

the Mid-Ocean Escort Force, and starting in May the RCN became fully responsible for the close escort of all trans-Atlantic convoys between Britain and New York—the main route. To undertake this with available resources, the size of trans-Atlantic convoys was dramatically increased, and the frequency of sailings reduced. The largest convoy of the war, HX.300 of 167 ships in nineteen columns spread over thirty square miles, carrying over a million tons of supplies, crossed the mid-Atlantic in July with a Canadian escort of one frigate and six corvettes.

The reorganization of escort duties in the spring of 1944 turned the North Atlantic into something of a Canadian lake, and again it was the corvette fleet that formed the backbone of the effort. The MOEF swelled to eight C groups by October 1944 and added a ninth in February 1945. Through the spring and summer of 1944 these groups were composed largely of one or two new frigates (which seem to have gone to C groups and support groups on a 50-50 basis), and a half-dozen modernized corvettes from the early building programs. However, by the end of the summer the new IE class began to appear in the MOEF in considerable numbers, and by the fall all of the Castle class were serving in C groups as well. By early 1945 virtually all of the RCN's IE corvettes were operating in the MOEF (by March only three of the thirty still in service were elsewhere) and—with the exception of five or six die-hards—the corvettes of the 1939-1940 and 1940-1941 programs were retired to inshore waters.

The greatest enemy of the late-war corvettes seems to have been the sea itself, and she scored no victory over them. U-boats, driven down by airpower, lurked menacingly in inshore waters and posed a latent threat to the main trade routes, but convoy after convoy sailed with little to distinguish their passing—much to the relief of all except the Germans. The IE class fought no great battles and sank no submarines. Their contribution, like that of their earlier counterparts in the trying days of 1941-1943, was that in simply being there they made possible the system which ultimately decided the war in the Atlantic. The last to commission, *Fergus*, sailed on her first operation in early February 1945 and was paid off only five months later. It should also be noted that the IE class underwent no major changes in appearance during their wartime careers.

The bulk of corvette action in 1944 involved those sent overseas to serve in Operation Neptune, the naval side of the D Day landings. The RCN provided 7 percent

of Neptune's naval forces and among the Canadian ships were nineteen corvettes. Four of these, *Lindsay*, *Louisburg*, *Mimico* and *Trentonian*, were IE class, the rest were old salts of the Atlantic war. They included the revised corvettes *Prescott*, *Calgary*, *Woodstock*, *Regina*, *Port Arthur* and *Kitchener*, the British-owned *Mayflower*, and eight other veterans of the first building program: *Alberni*, *Baddeck*, *Camrose*, *Lunenburg*, *Drumheller*, *Rimouski*, *Moose Jaw*, and *Summerside*. Theirs was beyond doubt the most hazardous work undertaken by any of Canada's corvettes. To escort the shipping required for the buildup, launching and support of the invasion required sailing in waters infested with mines, U-boats, motor torpedo boats (E-boats), destroyers and hostile aircraft. *Woodstock* and *Regina* commenced the new duties at the end of April, and by the end of May twelve were at work, with the remaining seven due shortly. In all, 28 percent of the corvettes that participated in Neptune were RCN.

In the assault phase of the D Day operation most Canadian corvettes were assigned to escort the blockships, concrete barges, breakwaters and sections of pontoons needed to build the artificial harbours (code-named Mulberries) to support the forces ashore. These units arrived on 7 and 8 June, with RCN corvettes providing the bulk of escorting forces for the Mulberry harbours. Only *Kitchener*, escorting a group of infantry landing ships, was off the beaches on the day of the landings. The rest of June was taken up with escorting support convoys. As Joseph Schull wrote in *The Far Distant Ships*, "They came under attack from E-boats on one or two occasions, air attacks were fairly frequent, and the danger of mines was ever present. On the whole, however, the veterans of the Atlantic convoy routes were rather disparaging in their comments on life in the big league. Monotony was with them eternally and excitement was rare." (p.327). By the end of June the corvettes had settled into a routine of escorting coastal convoys in the Channel from bases either at Milford Haven or Sheerness.

There was excitement nonetheless, and losses. *Alberni* got a break from routine in late July when she served on anti-submarine patrol off Sword Beach, anchoring at night as part of a barrier to the anchorage. On 26 July the anchorage was attacked by JU88 torpedo aircraft. One of these came in low over *Alberni*, whose crew opened fire with the bridge Oerlikons as the bomber passed over her forecastle at a height of 200 feet. The aircraft caught fire and crashed into the sea

*The after end of **Huntsville**. Her spacious quarterdeck is noteworthy for its almost complete lack of depth charges: just one short rail offset to starboard. The cylinders on the corners of her quarterdeck are smoke generators: the two canvas-covered guns on the raised platform are power-driven, twin 20-mm mountings. **Long Branch** lies astern in this November 1944 view.*

about 1000 yards away—the only aircraft destroyed by a Canadian corvette during the war.

The enemy got his revenge on *Alberni* a month later when she was torpedoed by *U 480* off the Isle of Wight. As with most other corvette losses, *Alberni* sank with frightening speed: within twenty-seconds of the explosion only the bow remained above the surface. As she sank rapidly she rolled over on men in the water and one of her boilers blew, increasing the list of missing to fifty-nine in all. Some crewmen credited their escape from *Alberni* to the few seconds of time saved because her forecastle had not yet been extended. *Alberni* was actually the second of the D Day corvettes to be lost. On 8 August *Regina* had been torpedoed after she stopped to assist a ship in her convoy which everyone thought had struck a mine. In fact, the merchantman had been the target of the first of two torpedos from *U 667*. The second struck *Regina*, probably near the bridge, since either her boilers or magazine were detonated by the torpedo's explosion. Whatever the cause, *Regina* was shattered in a tremendous explosion and sank in seconds. Ships nearby nonetheless recovered sixty-six of her crew.

The D Day corvettes sailed in UK waters for the balance of the war, escorting convoys and performing a host of essential, if often mundane, tasks. These operations claimed one final victim on 22 February 1945, when *Trentonian* was torpedoed by *U 1004*. The corvette was struck astern, probably by an acoustic torpedo, which opened the after part of the ship and flooded the engine room. Mercifully, *Trentonian* took her time to sink and the six dead among her crew were all killed by the explosion. She was the last Canadian corvette lost during the war and the only one of the RCN's IE corvettes to succumb to enemy action.

The inshore U-boat campaign which occupied the attention of the UK-based corvettes and support groups also had its counterpart in Canadian waters. As the range of U-boats was reduced by the loss of their French bases and by the need to travel submerged all the time to evade omnipresent Allied patrols, Canada's east coast was one of the few distant places Germany's submariners could reach. In the last half of 1944 and during the first four months of 1945 U-boats in Canadian waters accounted for a number of merchant ships and escorts. One of these losses was the corvette *Shawinigan*.

In late November 1944 *Shawinigan* found herself patrolling the Cabot Strait with the US Coast Guard cutter *Sassafras*, and taking turns escorting the Sydney-to-Port-aux-Basques ferry. At supper time on 24 November *Shawinigan* delivered the ferry to Port-aux-Basques and, after arranging a morning rendezvous, sailed for an independent patrol. The last person to see her was the captain of *U 1228*, who fired a single acoustic homing torpedo at the corvette early the next morning. Typically, the corvette sank with alarming speed: *U 1228*'s log records her disappearance almost as soon as the blast subsided. Once again the corvette's own depth charges (and possibly her boilers) fuelled the carnage. *Shawinigan*'s loss was verified the next day when wreckage and bodies were found off Cape North, Cape Breton Island. Further searches produced more scattered wreckage, but all that was ever recovered from *Shawinigan* were two Carley floats and six bodies.

By the end of the war in Europe on 18 May 1945 there were 114 corvettes remaining on active service in the RCN, from a total of 123 commissioned into Canadian service during the war: the largest class of warship ever to serve Canada. In a little less than five years they had escorted convoys as far south as Trinidad, north to Iceland, west to the tip of the Aleutian chain in the Pacific and east to the middle of the Mediterranean. They sank, or shared in the sinking, of fourteen enemy submarines, and downed one JU88. In the process ten of their number were destroyed by enemy action: 40 percent of the RCN's losses in escort vessels during the war. They escorted countless ships, rescued hundreds of sailors and by their mere presence saved the lives of hundreds more, and preserved hundreds of thousands of tons of merchant shipping for the Allied cause. As Admiralty Sir Dudley Pound, First Sea Lord of the British Admiralty observed, the Royal Canadian Navy solved the problems of the Atlantic convoys; and they did it very largely with corvettes.

Most corvettes of the first building program ended the war where they started: doing inshore escort based in Halifax. However, they present a very different picture in March 1945 from those shown alongside the same jetty in 1941 (see Chapter II). **Dundas** *is inboard,* **Chilliwack** *next to her and the rest are unidentified.*

The naval photographer captioned this shot, "HMCS **Barrie***, corvette, at play. June 1945."*

CHAPTER VI

Where Have All The Flowers Gone?

As the war in Europe ran down, Canadian planners prepared for the Pacific, where it looked as though the war with Japan would last well into 1946 or perhaps beyond. It was, however, a very different kind of naval war, one about the projection of military power by massive fleets. With the enormous weight of American seapower already in play against Japan by the end of 1944, and that from Britain moving east, there was no need for the little ships of the Atlantic war. Therefore the RCN planned in late 1944 to send only the best of its corvette fleet, the Castle class, to the Pacific as part of a Canadian Task Force that would be made up largely of cruisers and destroyers. Eight Castles were to help support the Task Force's operations, leaving a reserve of four in Canadian waters. However, the British decision not to send any corvettes whatever to the Pacific war meant that there was no point in the RCN developing maintenance and logistical support for a small number of corvettes. The Castles were then dropped from the plans for the Pacific. The end of the war in Europe in May 1945 thus brought an end to the corvettes' war as well.

Disposal of surplus and worn-out warships got underway quickly after the end of hostilities. Among the first to go were the ships which had remained British government property, including the eight survivors of the ten corvettes commissioned into the RCN in May 1941. Four of these, *Arrowhead*, *Eyebright*, *Hepatica*, and *Trillium*, sailed to the UK with reduced crews at the end of May 1945 as escort to HX.358. The balance, *Bittersweet*, *Fennel*, *Mayflower*, and *Snowberry*, were returned to British ports by the end of June. The vast majority of Canada's wartime fleet turned west for disposal. The process got underway in earnest in early June, when mid-ocean and western escort forces were disbanded. Corvettes from St John's and Halifax steamed to Sydney, NS, for de-storing, and then on to Sorel, Quebec, with partial crews, for paying off and handing over to the War Assets Corporation. There they lay, moored in clutches to buoys in the St Lawrence River, until bought for conversion to merchant use, sold to foreign navies or towed away for the final trip to the wrecker's yard.

The process of paying off the corvette fleet went quickly. By the end of July, ninety-four of the 113 surviving ships were de-commissioned. It took until April of 1946 to finish with the rest. *Brantford*, attached to the training base at Cornwallis, and two of the four corvettes of the first construction program based on the west coast, *Sudbury* and *Shediac*, were paid off in

*Corvettes as far as the eye can see: awaiting final disposal, Sydney, NS, in the summer of 1945. Identifiable are **Stellarton** and **Matapedia**, the latter still with steam up.*

August. *Nanaimo* was paid off at Esquimalt in September and *Moncton* followed in December 1945—the last of the first program to serve the RCN as a warship. All of the Castle class ships stayed in commission for some time after the defeat of Japan, but five had been decommissioned before the end of 1945. The rest of the Castles were disposed of in early 1946, the last to go being *Orangeville* on 12 April. *Woodstock*, which was used temporarily as a weather ship, was struck from active service in March 1946. *Sackville*, converted at the end of the war to a loop layer, a vessel built to lay and maintain the indicator cables on the bottom at the entrance to defended ports, was paid off and assigned to the reserve fleet in April 1946.

According to the navy's official history, forty-five of the discarded corvettes were sold for scrap, although by later accounts only forty-one of these actually went directly to the breakers' yards. Not surprisingly, most of those scrapped were from the first two construction programs: thirty-one of the first sixty-four and nine of the fifteen ships of the 1940-1941 program. Among this

number was *Snowberry*, used briefly as a target by the RN before being discarded. Only one of the RCN's Canadian-built Increased Endurance/Improved Bridge class, *Atholl*, and two of the four ex-RN IE/IB corvettes, *Forest Hill* and *Giffard*, went straight to the wrecker. All the others, including the Castles, found some postwar employment.

Fifty-two ex-RCN corvettes, including four returned to Britain at the end of the war, were sold for mercantile use. Many of these, particularly the late-war ships, were converted into coastal steamers. Their superstructure was usually stripped off and a new bridge built aft over the machinery, while the mess decks forward were converted into cargo space. As merchant vessels, these former Canadian corvettes sailed the oceans of the world, serving under the flags of Greece, France, Panama, Argentina, Cambodia, China (both Nationalist and Peoples' Republic), Bahamas, Spain, Ecuador, Morocco, Honduras, India, Canada, and others. Six stayed close to home, and three of these were subsequently lost to accident. *Fergus*, serving as a coastal steamer, was wrecked off Newfoundland in 1949, *West York* sank at Montreal in 1960, and *Huntsville* sank after a collision off Trois Rivières in 1960. The other three went less dramatically. *Sudbury*, which served as a salvage tug on the west coast, went to the wrecker in Victoria in 1967, while *Long Branch* was scuttled off Nova Scotia in 1966 at the end of her career. *Leaside*, stripped to a hulk, sank in Cook Inlet, Alaska, in 1978. A year later she was raised, towed to sea and scuttled.

Of the forty-six which went to foreign buyers for mercantile use, most had gone to the breakers by the end of the 1960s. Before doing so, five of them had been returned to naval service. *Norsyd* and *Beauharnois* went to the Mediterranean, where they evidently were used to smuggle Jews through the British blockade into Palestine. Later both entered the new Israeli navy and served until scrapped in 1956. *Barrie*, sold to Argentine interests in 1947, was taken over by the Argentine navy in 1957 and converted into a survey vessel. She was broken up in 1972. Of the five Castle class sold to Chinese interests, two—*Copper Cliff* and *Bowmanville*—fell to the new Peoples' Republic in 1948 and were refitted as warships. The other three were retained by Nationalist Chinese owners, two apparently also being refitted as warships. The ultimate fate of these ships remains a mystery.

Seventeen of those sold for merchant use, including twelve of the first program, were converted—sadly but appropriately enough—by Dutch, Danish, Norwegian and Honduran firms into whale-catchers. They survived in this role for many years. The seven whale-catchers owned by the Dutch were finally scrapped in 1965-1966. Eight corvettes sold to Honduran whalers changed ownership in the mid-1950s, going first to one Japanese firm and then another. As will be seen in their individual histories, all but one of these ships soldiered on in this role into the 1970s.

Apart from whaling or carrying cargo, the second major use for the ex-RCN corvettes was as warships, largely in South America. In all, including those reconverted to naval purposes as mentioned above, twenty-four corvettes saw postwar service in the navies of the world. Venezuela bought seven of the first construction program ships: *Algoma*, *Amherst*, *Battleford*, *Dunvegan*, *Kamsack*, *Oakville* and *Wetaskiwin*. *Amherst* was wrecked on her way to Venezuela in 1945 and *Battleford* was lost in 1949. The rest of the Venezuelan corvettes were scrapped by 1962. *Stellarton*, *Strathroy* and *Thorlock* went to the Chilean navy, and served into the late 1960s before being discarded. The Uruguayan Castle class *Montevideo*, ex-*Arnprior*, served as a training ship until 1975. The fate of the Chinese Castles restored to warships remains a mystery, and some may possibly still exist. However, for the moment, the corvettes of the Dominican Republic's navy win the honours for longevity. Apart from *Asbestos*, lost en route off Cuba, the late-war corvettes *Lachute*, *Louisburg (II)*, *Rivière du Loup*, *Belleville*, and *Peterborough* served the Republic into the 1970s. Three were scrapped in 1972, and the last two—*Louisburg* and *Lachute*—were being considered for repatriation to Canada for restoration when they were driven ashore by a hurricane in 1979 and wrecked. With the loss of these ships the last vestiges of a once large and important part of Canadian history were all but extinguished. By the 1980s there remained one—and apparently only one—of Canada's wartime fleet of 123 corvettes. *Sackville*.

Like many a survivor, *Sackville*'s preservation from the breaker's yard owed something to happy accident. She survived several close encounters with U-boats, including three in one day, the worst winters of the North Atlantic war and some of the grimmest of convoy battles, and was nearly sunk on at least one occasion by an acoustic torpedo. What finally took *Sackville* out of the shooting war was the failure of one of her Scotch Marine boilers. Over-zealous maintenance and some shoddy workmanship led to cracks in her number one boiler in August 1944, shortly after her modernization in Galveston, Texas. Temporary repairs made in the UK were unsuccessful, and she returned to Canada on one boiler. With the war all but won, there was little value in undertaking the enormous task of replacing the damaged boiler. But as an otherwise sound and up-to-date ship *Sackville* had uses. She spent a short spell as a training ship for the Officer School (HMCS *Kings*) in Halifax. Then in October 1944 it was decided to convert *Sackville* to a loop layer. The conversion included removal of her number one boiler and its replacement with a cable tank, replacement of the main armament with a windlass for the cables and the fitting of handling equipment. Her conversion was still in progress when the war ended in Europe, but by July she was ready for duty. From then until she was paid off in April 1946, *Sackville* removed cable fields off Halifax, Sydney and Saint John.

Sackville, *reconfigured as a loop layer in 1945, was transformed in the early 1950s into an oceanographic research vessel (as seen here). In the 1960s her after gun tub was replaced by a large laboratory.*

Lindsay *rebuilt as the coastal passenger steamer* **North Shore**.

Shediac, *converted for use as a whale-catcher, served under Dutch flag as Jooske W. Vinke, 1958-1966.*

Her ability to undertake a useful non-operational task proved to be *Sackville*'s salvation. She was neither sold or scrapped. Instead, she was assigned to the reserve fleet, where she recommissioned in 1950 as a depot ship. Final salvation came with the Cold War and the rising threat of Soviet submarines. To counter them effectively the RCN needed proper oceanographic surveys of Canadian waters. Thus in 1953, as a civilian-manned Canadian naval auxiliary vessel, *Sackville* started a career in oceanographic research. She might well have been discarded in the late 1950s, when the issue of her shaky remaining boiler was raised. The boiler issue was, in fact, closely linked with *Sackville*'s suitability for underwater sound testing. Defence scientists wanted her refitted with quieter diesel engines, the cost of which (including stripping out the original machinery) was estimated at about one million dollars—more than the original cost of the ship. Finding a replacement boiler was no easy task either. With all the first construction program now gone either to foreign fleets or the breaker's, the navy had no spare Scotch Marine boilers on hand. With her hull in excellent condition, and with an estimated fifteen years of hull

life left in 1957, her fire-tube boiler was refurbished and she sailed on.

Sackville's status as a research vessel was enhanced by a series of refits and additions. In 1961 a laboratory was constructed across the after end of the engine room casing, and in 1972 her forecastle was extended further aft to provide increased accommodation and her old bridge completely replaced. Although she remained DND property through all of this, her work was done largely for the Bedford Oceanographic Institute of Dartmouth, NS, and focused increasingly on the study of marine life. Finally, in December 1982, after forty-one years on the North Atlantic, she was retired from service.

A movement to find and preserve one of Canada's corvette fleet had been underway in the 1970s, when efforts were focused on obtaining a ship as little modified as possible. Interest therefore naturally centred on the two remaining corvettes of the Dominican navy. Surveys determined that these late-war ships were badly decayed by decades of hot, humid weather and poor maintenance: they broke easily when driven ashore by the hurricane of 1979. *Sackville*

*Warriors to the end, Cristobal Colon, **(ex-Lachute)** and Juan Alejandro Costa **(ex-Louisburg II)** of the Dominican navy, 1976. They were wrecked in a hurricane three years later.*

was the last of the many by the early 1980s. Although extensively modified, she was otherwise in excellent shape, and the momentum for her preservation was unstoppable.

In May 1983 *Sackville* was dedicated as the Canadian Naval Memorial by the Departments of Defence and Veterans Affairs. Restoration work began in June and the ship was formally transferred to the Canadian Naval Corvette Trust in October 1983. The Trust's plan was to restore *Sackville* to her late-war appearance, following the modernization of early 1944. As such she embodies all the improvements to the original corvette design: extended forecastle, modernized bridge, 20-mm and 2-pdr secondary armament, Hedgehog, Type 271 radar, and the boat and Carley float arrangement in accordance with late-war policy. As one of the first construction program, *Sackville* also retains the essential features that characterized the RCN adaptation of the original corvette design to particular Canadian needs. Her broad quarterdeck and square stern once carried minesweeping equipment, her after gun position stands at the very end of the engine room casing, and her galley sits jammed uneasily between the funnel and the bridge. As a monument to the corvette fleet, fate could not have made a happier choice.

Finding the necessary armament and equipment to restore *Sackville* to her 1944 appearance proved a difficult and often frustrating task, but by 1985—the year of the RCN's seventy-fifth anniversary celebrations—she had regained her old lines. That summer *Sackville* was moved to the Maritime Museum of the Atlantic, and opened to the public—a fitting memorial to that fleet of "far flung, storm-tossed little ships" that served Canada so well.

PART II: *THE SHIPS*

1939-1940 CANADIAN PROGRAM

AGASSIZ	K129	DRUMHELLER	K167	ORILLIA	K119
ALBERNI	K103	DUNVEGAN	K177	PICTOU	K146
ALGOMA	K127	EDMUNDSTON	K106	PRESCOTT	K161
AMHERST	K148	GALT	K163	QUESNEL	K133
ARVIDA	K113	KAMLOOPS	K176	RIMOUSKI	K121
BADDECK	K147	KAMSACK	K171	ROSTHERN	K169
BARRIE	K138	KENOGAMI	K125	SACKVILLE	K181
BATTLEFORD	K165	LETHBRIDGE	K160	SASKATOON	K158
BRANDON	K149	LÉVIS	K115	SHAWINIGAN	K136
BUCTOUCHE	K179	LOUISBURG	K143	SHEDIAC	K110
CAMROSE	K154	LUNENBURG	K151	SHERBROOKE	K152
CHAMBLY	K116	MATAPEDIA	K112	SOREL	K153
CHICOUTIMI	K156	MONCTON	K139	SUDBURY	K162
CHILLIWACK	K131	MOOSE JAW	K164	SUMMERSIDE	K141
COBALT	K124	MORDEN	K170	THE PAS	K168
COLLINGWOOD	K180	NANAIMO	K101	TRAIL	K174
DAUPHIN	K157	NAPANEE	K118	WETASKIWIN	K175
DAWSON	K104	OAKVILLE	K178	WEYBURN	K173

Displacement: 950 tons (standard)
Length Overall: 205'1"
Breadth: 33'1"
Draft: 8'3" forward; 13'5" aft (full load)
Machinery: 4-cyl. triple-expansion engine, 2,750 HP
2 Scotch marine boilers. Fuel: 230 tons
Top Speed: 16 knots Endurance: 3,450 n.m. @ 12 knots
Armament: one 4" BL Mk.IX; 2 twin 0.5" m.g.; 2 twin .303" m.g.; 2 (later 4) D.C. throwers; 2 rails; 40 (later 70) D.C.

The machine guns proved useless and were later replaced with a 2-pdr Mk.VIII pom-pom in the after gun tub and a single 20-mm Oerlikon on each bridge wing. Torch and Neptune nominees had their A/A armament further augmented by two 20-mm abreast each side of the after gun position.

Complement: 7 officers and 85-90 other ranks by war's end

NOTE: these ships were also initially fitted for minesweeping.

AGASSIZ

Builder: Burrard Dry Dock Co. Ltd., Vancouver, BC.
Launched 15.8.40. Period in Commission: 23.1.41-14.6.45.
Modernization: fo'c'sle extended at New York, 16.12.43-4.3.44
Fate: broken up at Moncton, NB, 1946.

▲ *Agassiz in 1942*

ALBERNI

Builder: Yarrows Ltd., Esquimalt, BC.
Launched: 22.8.40. Period in Commission: 4.2.41-21.8.44.
Particular Service: Operations Torch and Neptune.
Fate: torpedoed and sunk by *U 480* in the English Channel,
    21.8.44, with the loss of fifty-nine lives.

▼ *Alberni in 1944. She was lost before her fo'c'sle could be
extended.*

ALGOMA

Builder: Port Arthur [Ont.] Shipbuilding Co. Ltd.
Launched: 17.12.40. Period in Commission: 11.7.41-6.7.45.
Particular Service: Operation Torch.
Modernization: fo'c'sle extended at Liverpool, NS,
    30.12.43-15.4.44.
Postwar Career: to Venezuelan navy as *Constitución*,
    1945-1962.

▲ *Algoma* at Moville in 1941, wearing a good, if scabrous, example of disruptive camouflage.

AMHERST

Builder: Saint John [NB] Dry Dock & Shipbuilding Co. Ltd.
Launched: 4.12.40. Period in Commission: 5.8.41-16.7.45.
Modernization: fo'c'sle extended at Charlottetown, PEI,
    19.5-1.11.43.
Postwar Career: Sold to the Venezuelan navy in 1945 and
    renamed *Carabobo*. Wrecked on the Gaspé coast in
    December 1945 en route to Venezuela.

▼ *Amherst* in 1942

ARVIDA

Builder: Morton Engineering & Dry Dock Co., Quebec City.
Launched: 21.9.40. Period in Commission: 22.5.41-14.6.45.
Modernization: fo'c'sle extended at Baltimore, MD,
    24.1.44-8.4.44.
Postwar Career: became Spanish-flag merchant ship *La Ceiba*, 1950. Last noted in Lloyd's Register for 1953-54.

▲ *Arvida* on 5 September 1944

BADDECK

Builder: Davie Shipbuilding Co. Ltd., Lauzon, PQ.
Launched: 20.11.40. Period in Commission: 18.5.41-4.7.45.
Particular Service: Operations Torch and Neptune.
Modernization: fo'c'sle extended at Liverpool, NS,
    10.8-15.11.43.
Postwar Career: sold in 1946 for conversion to mercantile
    use, serving under the following names: *Efthalia* and *Yousuf Z. Alireza* (1947); *Yusouf* (1948); *Al Mansour* (1954); *Radwa* (1955); and *Evi* (1965).
Fate: lost ashore near Jedda, 11.3.66.
NOTE: Lloyd's Register carried her as *Yousuf Z. Alireza* until dropping her after 1965.

▼ *Baddeck* in the Channel, 10 June 1944

BARRIE

Builder: Collingwood [Ont.] Shipyards Ltd.
Launched: 23.11.40. Period in Commission:
    12.5.41-26.6.45.
Modernization: fo'c'sle extended at Liverpool, NS,
    17.3-17.7.44.
Postwar Career: became Argentinian *Gasestado*, 1947; to
    Argentine navy as survey vessel *Cap Canepa*, 1957-1972.

▲ *Barrie, 1943-1944*

BATTLEFORD

Builder: Collingwood [Ont.] Shipyards Ltd.
Launched: 15.4.41. Period in Commission: 31.7.41-18.7.45.
Particular Service: assisted in sinking *U 356*, 27.12.43.
Modernization: fo'c'sle extended at Sydney, NS, 8.4-31.7.44.
Postwar Career: to Venezuelan navy as *Libertad*, 1945.
Fate: wrecked, 12.4.49.

▼ *Battleford, 1943-1944*

BRANDON

Builder: Davie Shipbuilding Co. Ltd., Lauzon, PQ.
Launched: 29.4.41. Period in Commission: 22.7.41-22.6.45.
Modernization: fo'c'sle extended at Grimsby, UK,
    10.8-16.10.43.
Fate: broken up at Hamilton, Ont., 1945.

▲ *Brandon* in 1943

BUCTOUCHE

Builder: Davie Shipbuilding Co. Ltd., Lauzon, PQ.
Launched: 20.11.40. Period in Commission: 5.6.41-15.6.45.
Modernization: fo'c'sle extended at Saint John, NB,
    14.10.43-29.1.44.
Fate: broken up at Hamilton, Ont., 1949.

▼ *Buctouche* during workups, Bermuda, February 1944

CAMROSE

Builder: Marine Industries Ltd., Sorel, PQ.
Launched: 16.11.40. Period in Commission:
    30.6.41-22.7.45.
Particular Service: Operations Torch and Neptune. Took part
    in the sinking of *U 757*, 8.1.44.
Modernization: fo'c'sle extended at Pictou, NS,
    29.4-15.10.43.
Fate: broken up at Hamilton, Ont., 1947.

▲ *Camrose* in March 1945

CHAMBLY

Builder: Canadian Vickers Ltd., Montreal, PQ.
Launched: 29.7.40. Period in Commission:
    18.12.40-20.6.45.
Particular Service: assisted in sinking *U 501*, 10.9.41.
Modernization: fo'c'sle extended at Liverpool, NS,
    9.12.43-11.3.44.
Postwar Career: sold 1946; entered service as Dutch whaler
    Sonja Vinke, 1952.
Fate: arrived at Santander, Spain, in October 1966 for
    breaking up.

▼ *Chambly* in January 1945

CHICOUTIMI

Builder: Canadian Vickers Ltd., Montreal, PQ.
Launched: 16.10.40. Period in Commission:
    12.5.41-16.6.45.
Fate: broken up at Hamilton, Ont., 1946.

▲ *Chicoutimi* in April 1942

CHILLIWACK

Builder: Burrard Dry Dock Co. Ltd., Vancouver, BC.
Launched: 14.9.40. Period in Commission: 8.4.41-14.7.45.
Particular Service: assisted in sinking *U 356*, 27.12.42, and
    U 744, 6.3.44.
Modernization: fo'c'sle extended at Halifax, NS,
    12.4-10.10.43.
Fate: broken up at Hamilton, Ont., 1946.

▼ *Chilliwack* in June 1942

COBALT

Builder: Port Arthur [Ont.] Shipbuilding Co. Ltd.
Launched: 17.8.40. Period in Commission:
    25.11.40-17.6.45.
Modernization: fo'c'sle extended at Liverpool, NS,
    22.3-20.7.44.
Postwar Career: sold 1946; in service as Dutch whaler
    Johanna W. Vinke from 1953.
Fate: broken up at Cape Town in 1966.

▲ *Cobalt* in 1941, still without secondary armament

COLLINGWOOD

Builder: Collingwood [Ont.] Shipyards, Ltd.
Launched: 27.7.40. Period in Commission: 9.11.40-23.7.45.
Modernization: fo'c'sle extended at New York,
    19.10-14.12.43.
Fate: broken up at Hamilton, Ont., 1950.
NOTE: Collingwood was the first Canadian corvette to enter
    service.

▼ *Collingwood* in July 1942

DAUPHIN

Builder: Canadian Vickers Ltd., Montreal, PQ.
Launched: 24.10.40. Period in Commission:
    17.5.41-20.6.45.
Particular Service: Aleutian campaign.
Modernization: fo'c'sle extended at Pictou, NS, 22.4-5.9.43.
Postwar Career: sold in 1949 to become mercantile *Cortes*;
    renamed *San Antonio*, 1955. Last noted in Lloyd's
    Register for 1963-64.

▲ *Dauphin* in 1941, still without radar. Her camouflage is
unusual.

DAWSON

Builder: Victoria [BC] Machinery Depot.
Launched: 8.2.41. Period in Commission: 6.10.41-19.6.45.
Particular Service: Aleutian campaign.
Modernization: fo'c'sle extended at Vancouver,
    4.10.43-29.1.44.
Fate: broken up at Hamilton, Ont. in 1946.

▼ *Dawson* on 6 July 1942. Note the "tall" west-coast
pendant numbers.

DRUMHELLER

Builder: Collingwood [Ont.] Shipyards, Ltd.
Launched: 5.7.41. Period in Commission: 13.9.41-11.7.45.
Particular Service: took part in sinking *U 753*, 13.5.43.
    Operation Neptune.
Modernization: fo'c'sle extended at New York,
    17.11.43-15.1.44.
Fate: broken up at Hamilton, Ont., 1949.

▲ *Drumheller* in 1942

DUNVEGAN

Builder: Marine Industries Ltd., Sorel, PQ.
Launched: 11.12.40. Period in Commission: 9.9.41-3.7.45.
Modernization: fo'c'sle extended at Baltimore, MD,
    25.10-27.12.43.
Postwar Career: to Venezuelan navy as *Independencia*,
    1945-1953.

▼ *Dunvegan* ca 1943

EDMUNDSTON

Builder: Yarrows Ltd., Esquimalt, BC.
Launched: 22.2.41. Period in Commission: 21.10.41-16.6.45.
Modernization: fo'c'sle extended at Halifax, NS, 5.1-3.6.43.
Postwar Career: entered service in 1948 as *Amapala*. Last
    noted in Lloyd's Register for 1961-62.

▲ *Edmundston in 1945*

GALT

Builder: Collingwood [Ont.] Shipyards, Ltd.
Launched: 28.12.40. Period in Commission:
    15.5.41-21.6.45.
Modernization: fo'c'sle extended at New York, 26.2-8.5.44.
Fate: broken up at Hamilton, Ont., 1946.

▼ *Galt in 1944*

KAMLOOPS

Builder: Victoria Machinery Depot Co. Ltd., Victoria, BC.
Launched: 7.8.40. Period in Commission: 17.3.41-27.6.45.
Modernization: fo'c'sle extended at Charlottetown, PEI,
    20.12.43-25.4.44.
Fate: broken up, 1946.

▲ *Kamloops* in 1942 while serving as training ship to
*Cornwallis. The lamps on her funnel were used in
experiments designed to make the ship invisible
against background light.*

KAMSACK

Builder: Port Arthur [Ont.] Shipbuilding Co. Ltd.
Launched: 5.5.41. Period in Commission: 4.10.41-22.7.45.
Modernization: fo'c'sle extended at Baltimore, MD,
    3.1-14.3.44.
Postwar Career: served the Venezuelan navy as *Federación*,
    1945-1956.

▼ *Kamsack* in 1944

KENOGAMI

Builder: Port Arthur [Ont.] Shipbuilding Co. Ltd.
Launched: 5.9.40. Period in Commission: 29.6.41-9.7.45.
Modernization: fo'c'sle extended at Liverpool, NS,
    28.6-1.10.44.
Fate: broken up at Hamilton, Ont., 1950.

▲ *Kenogami, 1943-1944*

LETHBRIDGE

Builder: Canadian Vickers Ltd., Montreal, PQ.
Launched: 21.11.40. Period in Commission: 25.6.41-23.7.45.
Particular Service: New York-Guantanamo convoys.
Modernization: fo'c'sle extended at Sydney, NS,
    23.12.43-27.3.44.
Postwar Career: entered service as Dutch whaler *Nicolaas
    Vinke*, 1955.
Fate: arrived at Santander, Spain, in September 1966 to be
    broken up.

▼ *Lethbridge* at Sydney, NS, in March 1944 after fo'c'sle
    extension.

LÉVIS

Builder: George T. Davie & Sons Ltd., Lauzon, PQ.
Launched: 4.9.40. Period in Commission: 16.5.41-19.9.41.
Fate: torpedoed by *U 74*, 120 miles east of Cape Farewell,
   Greenland, 19.9.41, and sank the following day, with
   the loss of eighteen lives.

▲ *Lévis* sinking

LOUISBURG

Builder: Morton Engineering & Drydock Co. Ltd., Quebec City
Launched: 27.5.41. Period in Commission: 2.10.41-6.2.43.
Particular Service: Operation Torch.
Fate: sunk by Italian aircraft east of Oran, 6.2.43, with the
   loss of forty lives.
NOTE: *Louisburg* was the only Canadian corvette lost to an air
   attack.

▼ *Louisburg* on 19 October 1942

LUNENBURG

Builder: George T. Davie & Sons Ltd., Lauzon, PQ.
Launched: 10.7.41. Period in Commission: 4.12.41-23.7.45.
Particular Service: Operations Torch and Neptune.
Modernization: fo'c'sle extended at Birkenhead, UK,
    7.4-17.8.43.
Fate: broken up at Hamilton, Ont., 1946.

▲ *Lunenburg, probably in 1942*

MATAPEDIA

Builder: Morton Engineering & Drydock Co. Ltd., Quebec City.
Launched: 14.9.40. Period in Commission: 9.5.41-16.6.45.
Modernization: fo'c'sle extended at Liverpool, NS,
    14.10.43-3.2.44.
Fate: broken up at Hamilton, Ont., 1950.

▼ *Matapedia, 1942-1943*

MONCTON

Builder: Saint John [NB] Dry Dock & Shipbuilding Co. Ltd.
Launched: 11.8.41. Period in Commission:
    24.4.42-12.12.45.
Modernization: fo'c'sle extended at Vancouver, BC,
    8.5-7.7.44.
Postwar Career: entered service in 1955 as Dutch whaler
    Willem Vinke.
Fate: broken up at Santander, Spain, in 1966.

▲ *Moncton* in November 1943

MOOSE JAW

Builder: Collingwood [Ont.] Shipyards, Ltd.
Launched: 9.4.41. Period in Commission: 19.6.41-8.7.45.
Particular Service: took part in sinking *U 501*, 10.9.41.
    Operations Torch and Neptune.
Modernization: fo'c'sle extended at Liverpool, NS,
    19.12.43-25.3.44.
Fate: broken up at Hamilton, Ont., 1949.

▼ *Moose Jaw, 1942-1943*

MORDEN

Builder: Port Arthur [Ont.] Shipbuilding Co. Ltd.
Launched: 5.5.41. Period in Commission: 6.9.41-29.6.45.
Particular Service: sank *U 756*, 1.9.42.
Modernization: fo'c'sle extended at Londonderry, Ireland,
    3.12.43-29.1.44.
Fate: broken up at Hamilton, Ont., 1946.

▲ *Morden* in the spring of 1944

NANAIMO

Builder: Yarrows Ltd., Esquimalt, BC.
Launched: 28.10.40. Period in Commission:
    26.4.41-28.9.45.
Postwar Career: entered service in 1955 as Dutch whaler
    Rene W. Vinke.
Fate: broken up at Cape Town in 1966.

▼ *Nanaimo* on 6 July 1945

NAPANEE

Builder: Kingston [Ont.] Shipbuilding Co. Ltd.
Launched: 31.8.40. Period in Commission: 12.5.41-12.7.45.
Modernization: fo'c'sle extended at Montreal, PQ,
    21.5-19.10.3.
Fate: broken up at Hamilton, Ont., 1946.

▲ *Napanee* in 1942

OAKVILLE

Builder: Port Arthur [Ont.] Shipbuilding Co. Ltd.
Launched: 21.6.41. Period in Commission:
    18.11.41-20.7.45.
Particular Service: Caribbean. New York-Guantanamo
    convoys. Sank *U 94*, 28.8.42.
Modernization: fo'c'sle extended at Galveston, TX,
    22.12.43-29.3.44.
Postwar Career: to Venezuelan navy as *Patria*, 1945-1962.

▼ *Oakville* in 1942

ORILLIA

Builder: Collingwood [Ont.] Shipyards, Ltd.
Launched: 15.9.40. Period in Commission: 25.11.40-2.7.45.
Modernization: fo'c'sle extended at Liverpool, NS, 8.2-3.5.44.
Fate: broken up at Hamilton, Ont., 1951.

▲ *Orillia* on 12 July 1942

PICTOU

Builder: Davie Shipbuilding Co. Ltd., Lauzon, PQ.
Launched: 5.10.40. Period in Commission: 29.4.41-12.7.45.
Modernization: fo'c'sle extended at New York, 17.1-31.3.44.
Postwar Career: entered service in 1950 as Honduran whaler
    Olympic Chaser; changed hands in 1956 to become *Otori
    Maru No.7.*
Fate: cut down to a barge in 1963.

▼ *Pictou* in 1945

PRESCOTT

Builder: Kingston [Ont.] Shipbuilding Co. Ltd.
Launched: 7.1.41. Period in Commission: 26.6.41-20.7.45.
Particular Service: sank *U 163*, 13.3.43. Operations Torch
    and Neptune.
Modernization: fo'c'sle extended at Liverpool, NS,
    26.4-27.10.43.
Fate: broken up at Hamilton, Ont., 1951.

▲ *Prescott* at St. John's, 1942-1943

QUESNEL

Builder: Victoria Machinery Depot Co. Ltd., Victoria, BC.
Launched: 12.11.40. Period in Commission: 23.5.41-3.7.45.
Modernization: fo'c'sle extended at Pictou, NS,
    11.9-23.12.43.
Fate: broken up at Hamilton, Ont., 1946.

▼ *Quesnel* on 10 September 1942

RIMOUSKI

Builder: Davie Shipbuilding Co. Ltd., Lauzon, PQ.
Launched: 3.10.40. Period in Commission: 26.4.41-24.7.45.
Particular Service: Operation Neptune.
Modernization: fo'c'sle extended at Liverpool, NS,
    25.3-24.8.43.
Fate: broken up at Hamilton, Ont., 1950.

▲ *Rimouski* in July 1945

ROSTHERN

Builder: Port Arthur [Ont.] Shipbuilding Co. Ltd.
Launched: 30.11.40. Period in Commission:
    17.6.41-19.7.45.
Fate: broken up at Hamilton, Ont., 1946.

▼ *Rosthern* aground under unknown circumstances, likely in
    1942, as she has not yet been fitted with Type 271 radar.

SACKVILLE

Builder: Saint John [NB] Dry Dock & Shipbuilding Co. Ltd.
Launched: 15.5.41. Period in Commission: 30.12.41-8.4.46.
Modernization: fo'c'sle extended at Galveston, TX,
    6.3.-7.5.44. Refitted for loop-laying duties, 1944-1945,
    and radically rebuilt in 1968 for oceanographic duties,
    civilian-manned.
NOTE: acquired in 1982 by the Canadian Naval Corvette Trust
    and restored to her original appearance, *Sackville* is on
    permanent display at the Maritime Museum of the Atlantic,
    Halifax.

▲ *Sackville* in September 1944, as training ship for King's.

SASKATOON

Builder: Canadian Vickers Ltd., Montreal, PQ.
Launched: 6.11.40. Period in Commission: 9.6.41-25.6.45.
Modernization: fo'c'sle extended at Pictou, NS,
    18.12.43-1.4.44.
Postwar Career: served as a whaler from 1948, successively
    named *Tra los Montes*, *Olympic Fighter* (1950), *Otori Maru
    No.6* (1956), and *Kyo Maru No.20* (1961). Last noted in
    Lloyd's Register for 1978-79.

▼ *Saskatoon* ca. 1943

SHAWINIGAN

Builder: George T. Davie & Sons Ltd., Lauzon, PQ.
Launched: 16.5.41. Period in Commission:
    19.9.41-25.11.44.
Modernization: fo'c'sle extended at Liverpool, NS,
    12.3-14.6.44.
Fate: torpedoed and sunk with all hands in Cabot Strait by
    U 1228, 25.11.44.

▲ *Shawinigan* in 1942

SHEDIAC

Builder: Davie Shipbuilding Co. Ltd., Lauzon, PQ.
Launched: 29.4.41. Period in Commission: 8.7.41-28.8.45.
Modernization: fo'c'sle extended at Vancouver, BC,
    12.6-18.8.44.
Postwar Career: entered service in 1958 as Dutch whaler
    Jooske W. Vinke.
Fate: arrived at Santander, Spain, in September 1966 to be
    broken up.

▼ *Shediac* off Juan de Fuca Strait on 21 May 1944, soon
    after arriving on the west coast.

SHERBROOKE

Builder: Davie Shipbuilding Co. Ltd., Lauzon, QC.
Launched: 25.10.40. Period in Commission: 5.6.41-28.6.45
Modernization: fo'c'sle extended at Liverpool, NS,
    25.5-22.8.44.
Fate: broken up at Hamilton, Ont., 1947.

▲ *Sherbrooke* in July 1943

SOREL

Builder: Marine Industries Ltd., Sorel, PQ.
Launched: 16.11.40. Period in Commission:
    19.8.41-22.6.45.
Modernization: fo'c'sle extended at Dartmouth, NS,
    1.11.43-31.3.44
Fate: broken up.

▼ *Sorel* in 1944

SUDBURY

Builder: Kingston [Ont.] Shipbuilding Co. Ltd.
Launched: 31.5.41. Period in Commission:
    15.10.41-28.8.45.
Particular Service: Caribbean. New York-Guantanamo convoys.
Modernization: fo'c'sle extended at Vancouver, BC,
    14.2-10.5.44.
Postwar Career: served under her original name as a salvage
    tug, 1949-1967.
Fate: broken up at Victoria, BC, 1967.

▲ *Sudbury in November 1944*

SUMMERSIDE

Builder: Morton Engineering & Drydock Co. Ltd., Quebec City
Launched: 17.5.41. Period in Commission: 11.9.41-6.7.45.
Particular Service: Operations Torch and Neptune.
Modernization: fo'c'sle extended at Saint John, NB,
    12.4-25.9.43.
Fate: broken up at Hamilton, Ont., 1946.

▼ *Summerside in July 1942*

THE PAS

Builder: Collingwood [Ont.] Shipyards, Ltd.
Launched: 16.8.41. Period in Commission:
    21.10.41-24.7.45.
Particular Service: Caribbean. New York-Guantanamo convoys.
Fate: broken up at Hamilton, Ont., 1946.

▲ *The Pas* in St. Margaret's Bay, 1942

TRAIL

Builder: Burrard Dry Dock Co. Ltd., Vancouver, BC.
Launched: 17.10.40. Period in Commission:
    30.4.41-17.7.45.
Modernization: fo'c'sle extended at Liverpool, NS,
    13.7-23.10.44.
Fate: broken up at Hamilton, Ont., 1950.

▼ *Trail* at Argentia, Newfoundland, during the Atlantic Charter meeting of August 1941.

WETASKIWIN

Builder: Burrard Dry Dock Co. Ltd., Vancouver, BC.
Launched: 18.7.40. Period in Commission:
    17.12.40-19.6.45.
Modernization: fo'c'sle extended at Galveston, TX,
    18.12.43-6.3.44.
Postwar Career: to Venezuelan navy as *Victoria*, 1945-1962.

▲ *Wetaskiwin* in 1943

WEYBURN

Builder: Port Arthur [Ont.] Shipbuilding Co. Ltd.
Launched: 26.7.41. Period in Commission:
    26.11.41-22.2.43.
Particular Service: Operation Torch.
Fate: mined and sunk off Gibraltar, 22.2.43, with the loss of
    ten lives.

▼ *Weyburn* in May 1942

1939-1940 PROGRAM, BUILT FOR THE RN

ARROWHEAD	K145	HEPATICA	K159	SPIKENARD	K198
BITTERSWEET	K182	MAYFLOWER	K191	TRILLIUM	K172
EYEBRIGHT	K150	SNOWBERRY	K166	WINDFLOWER	K155
FENNEL	K194				

NOTE: Built in Canada for the Royal Navy, these ten were commissioned between October 1940 and February 1941, but transferred on loan to the RCN on 15 May 1941.

Their particulars were identical to the rest of the 1939-1940 Program, except that they were not fitted with minesweeping gear. Another distinction, conveniently obvious for visual identification, was the siting of the after gun tub amidships, rather than abaft the engine room skylight. This arrangement precluded the fitting of the mainmast initially found in other members of this program.

ARROWHEAD

Builder: Marine Industries Ltd., Sorel, PQ.
Launched: 8.8.40. Period in Commission: 15.5.41-27.6.45.
Modernization: fo'c'sle extended at Charleston, SC,
    12.41-2.42.
Postwar Career: returned to RN. Sold in 1947 for conversion
    to whaler *Southern Larkspur*.
Fate: broken up at Odense, Denmark, 1959.

▲ *Arrowhead* in June 1942

BITTERSWEET

Builder: Marine Industries Ltd., Sorel, PQ.
Launched: 12.9.40. Period in commission: 15.5.41-22.6.45.
Modernization: fo'c'sle extended at Charleston, SC,
    31.12.41.-3.42
Fate: returned to the RN. Broken up at Rosyth, 1946.

▼ *Bittersweet* picking up a towline from *Skeena*, May 1943

EYEBRIGHT

Builder: Canadian Vickers Ltd., Montreal, PQ.
Launched: 22.7.40. Period in Commission: 15.5.41-17.6.45.
Modernization: fo'c'sle extended at Charleston, SC,
    12.41-1.42.
Postwar Career: returned to the RN. Entered service in 1950
    as Dutch whaler *Albert W. Vinke*.
Fate: broken up at Cape Town in 1965.

▲ *Eyebright, 1942-1943*

FENNEL

Builder: Marine Industries Ltd., Sorel, PQ.
Launched: 20.8.40. Period in Commission: 15.5.41-12.6.45.
Particular Service: took part in the sinking of *U 744*, 6.3.44.
Modernization: fo'c'sle extended at New York, 7-9.42.
Postwar Career: returned to the RN and sold in 1946. Entered
    service in 1948 as Norwegian whaler *Milliam Kihl*.
Fate: arrived at Grimstad in November 1966 to be broken up.

▼ *Fennel in April 1945*

HEPATICA

Builder: Davie Shipbuilding Co. Ltd., Lauzon, PQ.
Launched: 6.7.40. Period in Commission: 15.5.41-27.6.45.
Particular Service: Caribbean.
Modernization: fo'c'sle extended at New York, 11.2-1.4.43.
Fate: returned to the RN. Broken up at Llanelly, Wales, 1948.

▲ *Hepatica, 1941-1942*

MAYFLOWER

Builder: Canadian Vickers Ltd., Montreal, PQ.
Launched: 3.7.40. Period in Commission: 15.5.41-31.5.45.
Particular Service: Operation Neptune.
Modernization: fo'c'sle extended at Charleston, SC,
    9.12.41-9.2.42
Fate: returned to the RN. Broken up at Inverkeithing, 1947.

▼ *Mayflower in Hvalfjord, 1941*

SNOWBERRY

Builder: Davie Shipbuilding Co. Ltd., Lauzon, PQ.
Launched: 8.8.40. Period in Commission: 15.5.41-8.6.45.
Particular Service: Caribbean. Assisted in sinking of *U 536*
    north of the Azores, 20.11.43.
Modernization: fo'c'sle extended at Charleston, SC,
    8.12.41-2.42
Fate: returned to the RN in 1945 and used in 1946 as a
    gunnery target off Portsmouth. Broken up in 1947 at
    Thornaby-on-Tees.

▲ *Snowberry in February 1944, after refit at Baltimore, MD*

SPIKENARD

Builder: Davie Shipbuilding Co. Ltd., Lauzon, PQ.
Launched: 10.8.40. Period in Commission: 15.5.41-10.2.42.
Fate: torpedoed and sunk by *U 136*, 10.2.42, five hundred
    miles west of Ireland, with the loss of fifty-seven lives.

Spikenard leaving Halifax in late fall, 1941

TRILLIUM

Builder: Canadian Vickers Ltd., Montreal, PQ.
Launched: 26.6.40. Period in Commission: 15.5.41-27.6.45.
Modernization: fo'c'sle extended at Galveston, TX,
16.4-23.6.42.
Postwar Career: sold in 1947 and entered service as
Honduran-flag whaler *Olympic Runner* in 1950, then *Otori Maru No.10* in 1956 and *Kyo Maru No.16* in 1959. Last noted in Lloyd's Register for 1972-73.

▲ **Trillium** *rescuing survivors of a merchantman sunk in convoy, ON.166, 22 February 1943.*

WINDFLOWER

Builder: Davie Shipbuilding Co. Ltd., Lauzon, PQ.
Launched: 4.7.40. Period in Commission: 15.5.41-7.12.41.
Fate: rammed and sunk in fog off the Grand Banks by Dutch
SS *Zypenberg*, 7.12.41, with the loss of twenty-six lives.

▼ **Windflower** *on builder's trials off Quebec City in the fall of 1940.*

122

1940-1941 SHORT-FORECASTLE PROGRAM

BRANTFORD	K218	MIDLAND	K220	TIMMINS	K223
DUNDAS	K229	NEW WESTMINSTER	K228	VANCOUVER	K240

All particulars and remarks are the same as for the 1939-1940 Program, except that these ships were not fitted for minesweeping and were built with extended bridge wings.

BRANTFORD

Builder: Midland [Ont.] Shipyards Ltd.
Launched: 6.9.41. Period in Commission: 15.5.42-17.8.45.
Postwar Career: entered service in 1950 as Honduran-flag whaler *Olympic Arrow*; in 1956 became *Otori Maru No.11* and, in 1961, *Kyo Maru No. 21*. Last noted in Lloyd's Register for 1972-73.

▲ *Brantford in 1945*

DUNDAS

Builder: Victoria [BC] Machinery Depot Co. Ltd.
Launched: 25.7.41. Period in Commission: 1.4.42-17.7.45.
Modernization: fo'c'sle extended at Montreal, PQ, 13.6-19.11.43.
Fate: broken up at Hamilton, Ont., 1946.

▼ *Dundas on 11 April 1942, a week after commissioning*

MIDLAND

Builder: Midland [Ont.] Shipyards, Ltd.
Launched: 25.6.41. Period in Commission:
    17.11.41-15.7.45.
Modernization: fo'c'sle extended at Galveston, TX,
    15.3-25.5.44.
Fate: broken up at Fort William, Ont., 1946.

▲ *Midland at Halifax, ca. May 1945*

NEW WESTMINSTER

Builder: Victoria [BC] Machinery Depot Co. Ltd.
Launched: 14.5.41. Period in Commission: 31.1.42-21.6.45.
Modernization: fo'c'sle extended at Sydney, NS,
    3.5-10.12.43.
Postwar Career: sold for commercial use in 1947 and
    registered as *Elisa* in 1950. Successively named *Portoviejo*
    (1952) and *Azua (1954)*.
Fate: sold in 1966 for breaking up at Tampa, FL.

▼ *New Westminster brand new—no radar, no A/A aft*

TIMMINS

Builder: Yarrows Ltd., Esquimalt, BC.
Launched: 26.6.41. Period in Commission: 10.2.42-15.7.45.
Modernization: fo'c'sle extended at Liverpool, NS,
    29.6-16.10.44.
Postwar Career: entered service in 1948 as the Honduran-flag
    Guayaquil.
Fate: foundered at Guayaquil, Ecuador, 3.8.60.

▲ *Timmins, likely in 1943*

VANCOUVER

Builder: Yarrows Ltd., Esquimalt, BC.
Launched: 26.8.41. Period in Commission: 20.3.42-26.6.45.
Particular Service: Aleutian campaign.
Modernization: fo'c'sle extended at Vancouver, 6-16.9.43.
Fate: broken up at Hamilton, Ont., 1946.

▼ *Vancouver at Esquimalt after her fo'c'sle extension was
completed in September 1943.*

1940-1941 REVISED PROGRAM

CALGARY	K231	KITCHENER	K225	REGINA	K234
CHARLOTTETOWN	K244	LA MALBAIE	K273	VILLE de QUÉBEC	K242
FREDERICTON	K245	PORT ARTHUR	K233	WOODSTOCK	K238
HALIFAX	K237				

Displacement:	1,015 tons (standard)	Breadth:	33'1"
Length Overall:	208'4"	Draft:	9'6" forward; 13'6" aft (full load)

Other particulars and remarks are the same as for the 1939-1940 Program, except that water-tube boilers were fitted instead of the Scotch marine type. Ships of subsequent programs were similarly fitted.

NOTE: these were the first Canadian corvettes to be built with extended fo'c'sles.

CALGARY

Builder: Marine Industries Ltd., Sorel, PQ.
Launched: 23.8.41. Period in Commission:
    16.12.41-19.6.45.
Particular Service: took part in the sinking of *U 536*,
    20.11.43. Operations Torch and Neptune.
Fate: broken up at Hamilton, Ont., 1951.

▲ *Calgary* in May 1944

CHARLOTTETOWN

Builder: Kingston [Ont.] Shipbuilding Co. Ltd.
Launched: 10.9.41. Period in Commission:
    13.12.41-11.9.42.
Fate: torpedoed and sunk by *U 517* near Cap Chat, PQ,
    11.9.42.

▼ *Charlottetown* in 1942

FREDERICTON

Builder: Marine Industries Ltd., Sorel, PQ.
Launched: 2.9.41. Period in Commission: 8.12.41-14.7.45.
Particular Service: Caribbean. New York-Guantanamo convoys.
Fate: broken up in 1946.

▲ *Fredericton* in November 1943

HALIFAX

Builder: Collingwood [Ont.] Shipyards Ltd.
Launched 4.10.41. Period in Commission: 26.11.41-12.7.45.
Particular Service: Caribbean. New York-Guantanamo convoys.
Postwar Career: sold for conversion to salvage vessel, 1946.

▼ *Halifax* in *1944, the first RCN corvette completed with a long fo'c'sle.*

KITCHENER

Builder: Marine Industries Ltd., Sorel, PQ.
Launched: 18.11.41. Period in Commission:
    28.6.42-11.7.45.
Particular Service: Operations Torch and Neptune. Was
    featured in the 1942 Hollywood film *Corvette K-225*.
Fate: broken up at Hamilton, Ont., 1949.

▲ *Kitchener in July 1942*

LA MALBAIE

Builder: Marine Industries Ltd., Sorel, PQ.
Launched: 25.10.41. Period in Commission:
    28.4.42-28.6.45.
Fate: broken up at Hamilton, Ont., 1951.

▼ *La Malbaie, likely in 1943*

PORT ARTHUR

Builder: Port Arthur [Ont.] Shipbuilding Co. Ltd.
Launched: 18.9.41. Period in Commission: 26.5.42-11.7.45.
Particular Service: Operations Torch and Neptune. Took part
    in the sinking of the Italian submarine *Tritone*, 19.12.43.
Fate: broken up at Hamilton, Ont., 1948.

▲ *Port Arthur, 1942-1943, with A/A armament augmented
for Torch.*

REGINA

Builder: Marine Industries Ltd., Sorel, PQ.
Launched: 14.10.41. Period in Commission: 22.1.42-8.8.44.
Particular Service: Operations Torch and Neptune. Sank the
    Italian submarine *Avorio*, 8.2.43.
Fate: torpedoed and sunk off Trevose Head, Cornwall, by
    U 667, 8.8.44.

▼ *Long thought to be* **Ville de Québec,** *this is almost
certainly* **Regina***. Date of photo would be spring, 1942.*

VILLE de QUÉBEC

Builder: Morton Engineering & Dry Dock Co., Quebec City.
Launched: 12.11.41. Period in Commission: 24.5.42-6.7.45.
Particular Service: Operation Torch. Sank *U 224*, 13.12.43.
Postwar Career: sold for mercantile use, 1946. Renamed
    Dispina (1946), *Dorothea Paxos* (1947), *Tanya* (1948),
    and *Medex* (1949). On Lloyd's Register until 1952.

▲ *Ville de Québec, 1942-1943*

WOODSTOCK

Builder: Collingwood [Ont.] Shipyards Ltd.
Launched: 10.12.41. Period in Commission: 1.5.42-27.1.45.
Particular Service: Operations Torch, Neptune.
Postwar Career: served 17.5.45-18.3.46 as a weather ship
    on the west coast. Sold in 1948 and entered service in
    1951 as Honduran-flag whaler *Olympic Winner*, *Otori Maru
    No.20*, 1956; *Akitsu Maru*, 1957.
Fate: broken up at Etajima, Japan, 1975.

▼ *Woodstock, likely when working up in June 1942. She has
    as yet no gunshield and no A/A armament.*

1942-1943 INCREASED ENDURANCE PROGRAM

ATHOLL	K15	HAWKESBURY	K415	OWEN SOUND	K340
COBOURG	K333	LINDSAY	K338	RIVIÈRE du LOUP	K357
FERGUS	K686	LOUISBURG (2ND)	K401	ST. LAMBERT	K343
FRONTENAC	K335	NORSYD	K520	TRENTONIAN	K368
GUELPH	K687	NORTH BAY	K339	WHITBY	K346

Displacement: 970 tons (standard)

Length Overall: 208'4"

Breadth: 33'1"

Draft: 8'10" forward; 13'3" aft (full load)

Machinery: 4-cyl. triple-expansion engine. 2,750 HP
Two water-tube boilers. Fuel: 338 tons. Pressurized boiler rooms eliminated the need for the large, distinctive ventilators grouped around the funnels of earlier corvettes.

Top Speed: 16 knots. Endurance: 7,400 n.m. @ 10 knots

Armament: One 4" QF Mk.XIX; single 20-mm on the bridge wings; in some cases a 2-pdr aft, in other cases 2 twin 20-mm; Hedgehog; 4 D.C. throwers, 2 rails. 100 D.C.

Complement: 7 officers, 90 other ranks.

ATHOLL

Builder: Morton Engineering & Dry Dock Co., Quebec City.
Launched: 4.4.43. Period in Commission: 14.10.43-17.7.45.
Fate: broken up at Hamilton, Ont., 1952.

▲ *Atholl* in 1944

COBOURG

Builder: Midland [Ont.] Shipyards Ltd.
Launched: 14.7.43. Period in Commission: 11.5.44-15.6.45.
Postwar Career: became mercantile *Camco*, 1947; *Dundas Kent*, 1951; *Puerto del Sol*, 1956.
Fate: burned and sank at New Orleans, LA, 1.7.71; raised and scrapped.

▼ *Cobourg* en route to the sea, May 1944

FERGUS

Builder: Collingwood [Ont.] Shipyards Ltd.
Launched: 30.8.44. Period in Commission:
    18.11.44-14.7.45.
Postwar Career: sold in 1945 and renamed *Camco II*, 1947;
    Harcourt Kent, 1948.
Fate: wrecked on Cape Pine, Newfoundland, 22.11.49.
NOTE: Fergus was the last Canadian corvette to be
    commissioned.

▲ *Fergus* during workups in Bermuda, January 1945

FRONTENAC

Builder: Kingston [Ont.] Shipbuilding Co. Ltd.
Launched: 2.6.43. Period in Commission: 26.10.43-22.7.45.
Fate: sold in October 1945.

▼ *Frontenac* in December 1944

GUELPH

Builder: Collingwood [Ont.] Shipyards Ltd.
Launched: 20.12.43. Period in Commission:
 9.5.44-27.6.45.
Postwar Career: converted for mercantile use in 1946
and for a time was in Panamanian-flag service under her
 original name. Renamed *Josephine Lanasa* in 1955
 and *Burfin* in 1956. Last noted in Lloyd's Register for
 1964-65.

Guelph *fitting out at Collingwood, 30 March 1944*

HAWKESBURY

Builder: Morton Engineering & Dry Dock Co., Quebec City.
Launched: 16.11.43. Period in Commission:
    14.6.44-10.7.45.
Postwar Career: became the Cambodian-flag *Campuchea* in
    1950.
Fate: broken up at Hong Kong in 1956.

▲ *Hawkesbury* in 1944

LINDSAY

Builder: Midland [Ont.] Shipyards Ltd.
Launched: 4.6.43. Period in Commission: 15.11.43-18.7.45.
Particular Service: Operation Neptune.
Postwar Career: sold for commercial use in 1946 and
    renamed *North Shore*; in 1961 renamed *Lemnos* under
    Greek flag.

▼ *Lindsay* in 1944

LOUISBURG (II)

Builder: Morton Engineering & Dry Dock Co., Quebec City.
Launched: 13.7.43. Period in Commission:
    13.12.43-25.6.45.
Particular Service: Operation Neptune.
Postwar Career: to Dominican navy as *Juan Alejandro Acosta*,
    1947.
Fate: decommissioned in 1978, and driven ashore in a
    hurricane, 31.8.79.

▲ *Louisburg* celebrating VE Day, 8 May 1944

NORSYD

Builder: Morton Engineering & Dry Dock Co., Quebec City.
Launched: 31.7.43. Period in Commission:
    22.12.43-25.6.45.
Postwar Career: entered mercantile service as *Balboa*, 1948.
    To Israeli navy in 1950 as *Haganah*.
Fate: broken up in 1956.

▼ *Norsyd*, *likely in 1944*

NORTH BAY

Builder: Collingwood [Ont.] Shipyards Ltd.
Launched: 27.4.43. Period in Commission: 25.10.43-1.7.45.
Postwar Career: sold in 1946 for mercantile use, becoming
Bahamian-flag *Kent County II*. Renamed *Galloway Kent*,
1950, and *Bedford II*, 1951. Last noted in Canadian
registry, 1959.

▲ *North Bay* at Montreal in November 1943

OWEN SOUND

Builder: Collingwood [Ont.] Shipyards Ltd.
Launched: 15.6.43. Period in Commission:
17.11.43-19.7.45.
Particular Service: assisted in the destruction of *U 843*,
10.3.44.
Postwar Career: sold in 1945 to become the Greek-flag
Cadio. Last noted in Lloyd's Register for 1967-68.

▼ *Owen Sound* in 1945

RIVIÈRE du LOUP

Builder: Morton Engineering & Dry Dock Co., Quebec City.
Launched: 2.7.43. Period in Commission: 21.11.43-2.7.45.
Postwar Career: to Dominican navy in 1947 as *Juan Bautista Maggiolo.*
Fate: broken up in 1972.

▲ *Rivière du Loup, likely in 1944*

ST. LAMBERT

Builder: Morton Engineering & Dry Dock Co., Quebec City.
Launched: 6.11.43. Period in Commission: 27.5.44-20.7.45.
Postwar Career: became the Panamanian-flag *Chrysi Hondroulis* in 1946, and the Greek *Loula* in 1955 and *Stefanos III* in 1958. Last noted in Lloyd's Register for 1964-65.
NOTE: Marine News, however, reports her as having been wrecked sixty miles west of Rhodes, 4.4.64, as *Chrysi Hondroulis.*

▼ *St. Lambert in 1944*

TRENTONIAN

Builder: Kingston [Ont.] Shipbuilding Co. Ltd.
Launched: 1.9.43. Period in Commission: 1.12.43-22.2.45.
Particular Service: Operation Neptune.
Fate: torpedoed and sunk SE of Falmouth by *U 1004*,
    22.2.45.
NOTE: The only late-war corvette sunk by enemy action.

▲ *Trentonian* during workups in Bermuda, February 1944

WHITBY

Builder: Midland [Ont.] Shipyards Ltd.
Launched: 18.9.43. Period in Commission: 6.6.44-16.7.45.
Postwar Career: sold in 1946 for merchant service, reportedly
    under the name of *Bengo*.

▼ *Whitby* on Georgian Bay, Ont., 1944

1943-1944 INCREASED ENDURANCE PROGRAM

ASBESTOS	K358	MERRITTONIA	K688	STELLARTON	K457
BEAUHARNOIS	K540	PARRY SOUND	K341	STRATHROY	K455
BELLEVILLE	K332	PETERBOROUGH	K342	THORLOCK	K394
LACHUTE	K440	SMITHS FALLS	K345	WEST YORK	K369

NOTE: all particulars and remarks are the same as for the 1942-1943 Program except that most, if not all, were fitted with 2 twin 20-mm and 2 single 20-mm A/A, lacking the 2-pdr.

ASBESTOS

Builder: Morton Engineering & Dry Dock Co., Quebec City.
Launched: 22.11.43. Period in Commission: 16.6.44-8.7.45.
Fate: sold in 1947 to the Dominican navy but wrecked en
    route. Salved and broken up at New Orleans, LA, in 1949.

▲ *Asbestos* in 1944

BEAUHARNOIS

Builder: Morton Engineering & Dry Dock Co., Quebec City.
Launched: 11.5.44. Period in Commission: 25.9.44-12.7.45.
Postwar Career: sold in 1946 to become mercantile *Colon*.
    Acquired in 1950 by the Israeli navy as *Wedgwood*.
Fate: broken up in Israel in 1956.

▼ *Beauharnois* in the St Lawrence on 25 September 1944,
the day she was commissioned.

BELLEVILLE

Builder: Kingston [Ont.] Shipbuilding Co. Ltd.
Launched: 17.6.44. Period in Commission: 19.10.44-5.7.45.
Postwar Career: to Dominican navy in 1947 as *Juan Bautista Cambiaso.*
Fate: broken up in 1972.

▲ *Belleville* dressed overall for a visit to her namesake town, 23 October 1944.

LACHUTE

Builder: Morton Shipbuilding & Dry Dock Co., Quebec City.
Launched: 9.6.44. Period in Commission: 26.10.44-10.7.45.
Postwar Career: to Dominican navy as *Colon,* 1947.
Fate: wrecked in a hurricane, 31.8.79.

▼ *Lachute* in March 1945

MERRITTONIA

Builder: Morton Shipbuilding & Dry Dock Co., Quebec City.
Launched: 24.6.44. Period in Commission:
    10.11.44-11.7.45.
Fate: sold for mercantile use in 1945 but wrecked that 30
    November on the Nova Scotia coast.

▲ *Merrittonia* in 1945

PARRY SOUND

Builder: Midland [Ont.] Shipyards Ltd.
Launched: 13.11.43. Period in Commission:
    30.8.44-10.7.45.
Postwar Career: entered service in 1950 as Honduran-flag
    whaler *Olympic Champion*; *Otori Maru No.15*, 1956;
    Kyo Maru No.22, 1961. Last noted in Lloyd's Register for
    1978-79.

▼ *Parry Sound* on Georgian Bay, Ont., in the summer of 1944

PETERBOROUGH

Builder: Kingston [Ont.] Shipbuilding Co. Ltd.
Launched: 15.1.44. Period in Commission: 1.6.44-19.7.45.
Postwar Career: to Dominican navy in 1947 as *Gerardo Jansen*.
Fate: disposed of for scrap in 1972.

▲ *Peterborough* in 1944

SMITHS FALLS

Builder: Kingston [Ont.] Shipbuilding Co.
Launched: 19.8.44. Period in Commission: 28.11.44-8.7.45.
Postwar Career: entered service in 1950 as Honduran-flag whaler *Olympic Lightning*; *Otori Maru No.16*, 1956; *Kyo Maru No.23*, 1961. Last noted in Lloyd's Register for 1977-78.

▼ *Smiths Falls* in February 1945

STELLARTON

Builder: Morton Engineering & Dry Dock Co., Quebec City.
Launched: 27.4.44. Period in Commission: 29.9.44-1.7.45.
Postwar Career: to Chilean navy as *Casma*, 1946.
Fate: broken up in 1969.

▲ *Stellarton* in 1945

STRATHROY

Builder: Midland [Ont.] Shipyards Ltd.
Launched: 15.6.44. Period in Commission:
    20.11.44-12.7.45.
Postwar Career: to Chilean navy as *Chipana*, 1946.
Fate: broken up in 1969.

▼ *Strathroy* in 1944

THORLOCK

Builder: Midland [Ont.] Shipyards Ltd.
Launched: 15.5.44. Period in Commission:
    13.11.44-15.7.45.
Postwar Career: to Chilean navy as *Papudo*, 1946.
Fate: sold for scrap in 1967.

▲ *Thorlock* *while working up in Bermuda, January 1945*

WEST YORK

Builder: Midland [Ont.] Shipyards Ltd.
Launched: 25.1.44. Period in Commission: 6.10.44-9.7.45.
Postwar Career: became mercantile *Guatemala*, 1946;
    Moulay Bouchaib, 1946; *Espresso*, 1953; *Federal Express*,
    1960.
Fate: sunk in collision at Montreal, 5.5.60. After part was
    raised and broken up later that year.

▼ *West York* *in May 1945*

BRITISH-BUILT
INCREASED ENDURANCE CORVETTES

| FOREST HILL | K486 | LONG BRANCH | K487 | MIMICO | K485 |
| GIFFARD | K402 | | | | |

These four were acquired at the end of 1943, in exchange for four Canadian-built Algerine class minesweepers. Their particulars were identical to those of the RCN's 1942-1943 Program, but with widely varying A/A armament.

FOREST HILL

Builder: Ferguson Bros. Ltd., Port Glasgow, Scotland.
Launched as HMS *Ceanothus*, 30.8.43.
Period in Commission: 1.12.43-9.7.45.
Fate: broken up at Hamilton, Ont., 1948.

▲ *Forest Hill* in December 1943

GIFFARD

Builder: Alexander Hall & Co. Ltd., Aberdeen, Scotland.
Launched as HMS *Buddleia*, 19.6.43.
Period in Commission: 10.11.43-5.7.45.
Fate: broken up at Hamilton, Ont., 1952.

▼ *Giffard* in 1945

LONG BRANCH

Builder: A. & J. Inglis Ltd., Glasgow, Scotland.
Launched as HMS *Candytuft*, 28.9.43.
Period in Commission: 5.1.44-17.6.45
Postwar Career: became mercantile *Rexton Kent II*, 1947.
Fate: scuttled off the east coast of Canada in 1966.

▲ *Long Branch* in 1944

MIMICO

Builder: John Crown & Sons Ltd., Sunderland, UK.
Launched as HMS *Bulrush*, 11.10.43.
Period in Commission: 8.2.44-18.7.45.
Postwar Career: entered service as whaler *Olympic Victor*,
    1950; *Otori Maru No.12*, 1956; *Kyo Maru No.25*, 1962.
    Last noted in Lloyd's Register for 1977-78.

▼ *Mimico* in 1944

CASTLE CLASS CORVETTES, BRITISH-BUILT

ARNPRIOR	K494	HUMBERSTONE	K497	ORANGEVILLE	K491
BOWMANVILLE	K493	HUNTSVILLE	K499	PETROLIA	K498
COPPER CLIFF	K495	KINCARDINE	K490	ST. THOMAS	K488
HESPELER	K489	LEASIDE	K492	TILLSONBURG	K496

Displacement: 1,010 tons (standard)

Length Overall: 251'9"

Breadth: 36'8"

Draft: 10' mean (full load)

Fuel: 480 tons

Machinery: 4-cyl. TE, 2,750 HP engine. Two water-tube boilers

Top Speed: 16.5 knots.

Endurance: 9,500 n.m. @ 10 knots

Armament: One 4" QF Mk.XIX; 2 twin 20-mm; 2 single 20-mm; 2 D.C. throwers, 1 rail, 15 D.C.s; 1 Squid mortar

Complement: 8 officers, 112 other ranks

NOTE: these were acquired in 1944, in exchange for twelve Canadian-built Algerine class minesweepers.

ARNPRIOR

Builder: Harland & Wolff Ltd., Belfast.
Launched 8.2.44 as HMS *Rising Castle*.
Period in Commission: 8.6.44-14.3.46.
Postwar Career: to the Uruguayan navy as *Montevideo*,
    serving as a training ship 1946-1975.

▲ *Arnprior* in 1944

BOWMANVILLE

Builder: Wm. Pickersgill & Sons Ltd., Sunderland.
Launched 26.1.44 as HMS *Nunney Castle*.
Period in Commission: 28.9.44-15.2.46.
Postwar Career: sold mercantile in 1947, to become the
    Chinese-flag *Ta Shun*, soon afterward renamed *Yuan Pei*.
    Taken over and rearmed by the Communist Chinese
    government and renamed *Kuang Chou*, she is thought to
    have served as late as 1982.

▼ *Bowmanville* in October 1944

COPPER CLIFF

Builder: Blyth Shipbuilding & Dry Dock Co., Blyth.
Launched 24.2.44 as HMS *Hever Castle*.
Period in Commission: 25.7.44-21.11.45.
Postwar Career: sold in 1947, she became the Chinese-flag
    Ta Lung, soon afterward renamed *Wan Lee*. Taken over
    by the Communist Chinese government in 1949 and
    rearmed, she is thought to have remained in service
    into the 1960s.

▲ *Copper Cliff* in 1944

HESPELER

Builder: Henry Ltd., Leith.
Launched 13.11.43 as HMS *Guildford Castle*.
Period in Commission: 28.2.44-15.11.45.
Particular Service: assisted in sinking *U 484*, 9.9.44.
Postwar Career: sold in 1946 to become the mercantile
    Chilcotin. In 1958 became the Liberian-flag *Stella Maris* and,
    in 1965, the Greek *Westar*.
Fate: gutted by fire in the Mediterranean, 28.1.66, and
    broken up at La Spezia, Italy.

▼ *Hespeler* in 1944

HUMBERSTONE

Builder: A. & J. Inglis Ltd., Glasgow.
Launched 12.4.44 as HMS *Norham Castle*.
Period in Commission: 6.9.44-17.11.45.
Postwar Career: sold in 1946, becoming the Chinese-flag
    Taiwei. She subsequently bore the names *Chang Chen*, *San
    Blas* and *South Ucun*.
Fate: broken up at Hong Kong in 1959.

▲ *Humberstone* in 1945

HUNTSVILLE

Builder: Ailsa Shipbuilding Co. Ltd., Troon.
Launched 24.2.44 as HMS *Woolvesey Castle*.
Period in Commission: 6.6.44-15.2.46.
Postwar Career: sold in 1946 and entered mercantile service
    in 1947 as *Wellington Kent*. Renamed *Belle Isle II* in 1951.
Fate: sunk in collision off Trois Rivières, 19.8.60.

▼ *Huntsville* in 1945

KINCARDINE

Builder: Smith's Dock Co., Smith's Dock-on-Tees.
Launched 26.1.44 as HMS *Tamworth Castle*.
Period in Commission: 19.6.44-27.2.46.
Postwar Career: sold to the French government in 1946 and
     resold the following year to become the Moroccan-flag
     Saada.

▲ *Kincardine in 1944*

LEASIDE

Builder: Smith's Dock Co., Smith's Dock-on-Tees
Launched 10.3.44 as HMS *Walmer Castle*.
Period in Commission: 21.8.44-16.11.45.
Postwar Career: sold in 1946 and converted to mercantile
     Coquitlam. Renamed *Glacier Queen* in 1950 and stripped for
     use as a floating restaurant.
Fate: sank in Cook Inlet, Alaska, 8.11.78, but was raised,
     towed to sea and scuttled in January 1979.

▼ *Leaside in September 1944*

ORANGEVILLE

Builder: Henry Robb Ltd., Leith.
Launched 26.1.44 as HMS *Hedingham Castle*.
Period in Commission: 24.4.44-12.4.46.
Postwar Career: sold in 1946 to become the Chinese-flag *Ta Tung*. Taken over in 1951 by the Nationalist Chinese government, rearmed and renamed *Te-An*. May have survived into the mid-1960s.

▲ *Orangeville on 27 April 1944*

PETROLIA

Builder: Harland & Wolff Ltd., Belfast.
Launched 24.2.44 as HMS *Sherborne Castle*.
Period in Commission: 29.6.44-8.3.46.
Postwar Career: sold to New York owners and renamed *Maid of Athens*, but entered Indian registry in 1947 as *Bharatlaxmi*.
Fate: broken up at Bombay in 1965. Her engine reportedly went to a consort, *Bharatdeepak*.

▼ *Petrolia in July 1944*

ST. THOMAS

Builder: Smith's Dock Co., Smith's Dock-on-Tees.
Launched 28.12.43 as HMS *Sandgate Castle*.
Period in Commission: 4.5.44-22.11.45.
Particular Service: sank *U 877*, 27.12.44.
Postwar Career: sold in 1946 to become S.S. *Camosun*.
　　Renamed *Chilcotin* in 1958 and, later that year, *Yukon Star*.
Fate: broken up in Taiwan in 1974 after several years' layup.

▲ *St. Thomas, 1944-1945*

TILLSONBURG

Builder: Ferguson Bros., Port Glasgow.
Launched 12.2.44 as HMS *Pembroke Castle*.
Period in Commission: 29.6.44-15.2.46.
Postwar Career: sold in 1946 to become the Chinese-flag *Ta Ching*. Renamed *Chiu Chin* in 1947, and in 1951 was taken over by the Nationalist Chinese government and renamed *Kao-An*. Like her sister, the former *Orangeville,* she may have survived in this role until the mid-1970s.

▼ *Tillsonburg in 1944*

APPENDIX I
PENDANT NUMBERS ("K" Superior)

K15	Atholl	K152	Sherbrooke	K191	Mayflower	K358	Asbestos
101	Nanaimo	153	Sorel	194	Fennel	368	Trentonian
103	Alberni	154	Camrose	198	Spikenard	369	West York
104	Dawson	155	Windflower	218	Brantford	394	Thorlock
106	Edmundston	156	Chicoutimi	220	Midland	401	Louisburg (II)
110	Shediac	157	Dauphin	223	Timmins	402	Giffard
112	Matapedia	158	Saskatoon	225	Kitchener	415	Hawkesbury
113	Arvida	159	Hepatica	228	New Westminster	440	Lachute
115	Lévis (I)	160	Lethbridge	229	Dundas	455	Strathroy
116	Chambly	161	Prescott	231	Calgary	457	Stellarton
118	Napanee	162	Sudbury	233	Port Arthur	485	Mimico
119	Orillia	163	Galt	234	Regina	486	Forest Hill
121	Rimouski	164	Moose Jaw	237	Halifax	487	Long Branch
124	Cobalt	165	Battleford	238	Woodstock	488	St. Thomas
125	Kenogami	166	Snowberry	240	Vancouver	489	Hespeler
127	Algoma	167	Drumheller	242	Ville de Québec	490	Kincardine
129	Agassiz	168	The Pas	244	Charlottetown	491	Orangeville
131	Chilliwack	169	Rosthern	245	Fredericton	492	Leaside
133	Quesnel	170	Morden	273	La Malbaie	493	Bowmanville
136	Shawinigan	171	Kamsack	332	Belleville	494	Arnprior
138	Barrie	172	Trillium	333	Cobourg	495	Copper Cliff
139	Moncton	173	Weyburn	335	Frontenac	496	Tillsonburg
141	Summerside	174	Trail	338	Lindsay	497	Humberstone
143	Louisburg (I)	175	Wetaskiwin	339	North Bay	498	Petrolia
145	Arrowhead	176	Kamloops	340	Owen Sound	499	Huntsville
146	Pictou	177	Dunvegan	341	Parry Sound	520	Norsyd
147	Baddeck	178	Oakville	342	Peterborough	540	Beauharnois
148	Amherst	179	Buctouche	343	St. Lambert	686	Fergus
149	Brandon	180	Collingwood	345	Smiths Falls	687	Guelph
150	Eyebright	181	Sackville	346	Whitby	688	Merrittonia
151	Lunenburg	182	Bittersweet	357	Rivière du Loup		

APPENDIX II

OPERATIONAL STATUS CHARTS

These charts are reproduced from *The Ships of Canada's Naval Forces, 1910-1985*, with the concurrence of its co-author, John Burgess. They show the assigned command and operational status, by month, for each of the corvettes of the RCN during the Second World War, comprising, in effect, a capsule history of each.

In order to compress this amount of information into the space available, the assigned command and operational status are represented by combinations of letters and numerals, to a maximum of three per space, arranged in two lines opposite the name of each ship. The top line represents the command or group to which the ship was assigned in each month, while the bottom line shows its operational status.

Referring, for example, to the corvette *Agassiz* for the month of August 1941, "19N" signifies that the ship was a unit of Escort Group 19 of Newfoundland Escort Force, based at St. John's. In the bottom line, "O" signifies that the ship was operational, escorting convoys between St. John's and Iceland.

It will be appreciated that there are limits to the extent to which such a condensation can be achieved, but it has been done in such a way as to cause minimum distortion of the ships' histories. This may best be illustrated by two further examples.

The corvette *Beauharnois* arrived in Bermuda from Halifax for workups on 8 November 1944, and departed 30 November, making two days' passage each way. She is therefore identified operationally that month as "WUB," that being how she was principally employed.

In the case of *Wetaskiwin*, who left Esquimalt for Halifax on 17 March 1941, arriving 13 April, the greater part of the month's passage took place in March, the "O/P" symbol thus appearing under that month.

KEY TO OPERATIONAL STATUS CHARTS

Note: in the case of number/letter combinations, the symbol is listed alphabetically by the letter.

TOP LINE

Symbol	Command	H.Q.
AT	Atlantic Coast Command, unallocated Later NW Atlantic Command, unallocated	Halifax, NS
A-3	EG A-3, MOEF, Newfoundland Command	St. John's, Nfld.
C-1 to C-9	EG C-3 to C-9, RCN (MOEF), Western Approaches Command, Londonderry	Londonderry and St. John's
CN	Commander, North-West Sea Frontier (USN) For duty in Aleutians invasion	Kodiak, AK
ES	Commander, Eastern Sea Frontier (USN). For New York-Guantanamo convoys	New York, NY
GE	Gulf Escort Force. For Gulf and St. Lawrence and Quebec-Sydney convoys	Gaspé, PQ
GF	Gaspé Force, unallocated. For Gulf convoys	Gaspé, PQ
26G	26th EG, Gibraltar Escort Force, Western Mediterranean Fleet (RCN)	Gibraltar
27G	27th EG, Gibraltar Escort Force, Western Mediterranean Fleet (RCN)	Gibraltar

62G	62nd EG, Gibraltar Escort Force, Western Mediterranean Fleet (RCN)	Gibraltar
HA	Halifax Force. For AH-HA (Halifax-Aruba) tanker convoys	Halifax, NS
HL	Halifax Local Defence Force. For Western Local Escort duties	Halifax, NS
HN	Halifax Force. For northern waters	Halifax, NS
HQ	Halifax Force. For NL-LN (Quebec-Labrador) convoys	Halifax, NS
HT	Halifax Tanker Escort Force. For HT-TH (Halifax-Trinidad) convoys	Halifax, NS
HX	Halifax Force	Halifax, NS
41H	41st EG, Plymouth Command (RCN) Ships under F.O.I.C., Milford Haven	Milford Haven, Wales
4-I	4th EG, Iceland Command (RN)	Reykjavik
6-L	6th EG, Western Approaches Command, Londonderry. RCN support group	Londonderry
25L	25th EG, Western Approaches Command, Londonderry. RCN support force, 1944-1945	Londonderry
26L	26th EG, Western Approaches Command, Londonderry. RCN support force, 1944-1945	Londonderry
27L	27th EG, Western Approaches Command, Londonderry (RCN)	Londonderry
62L	62nd EG, Western Approaches Command, Londonderry (RCN)	Londonderry
41M	41st EG, Plymouth Command (RN)	Plymouth
NC	New construction, Atlantic Coast Command New ship working up	Halifax, NS
NF	Newfoundland, unallocated (RCN). Mid-ocean escort group	St. John's, Nfld.
NO	Nore Command, unallocated (RN). Under N.O.I.C., Sheerness	Sheerness, UK
14N to 25N	14th to 25th EG, Newfoundland Escort Force. Mid-ocean escort groups	St. John's, Nfld.
N-1 to N-19	Task Units 4.1.1. to 4.1.19, later 24.1.1 to 24.1.19. Precursors of EG 1 to 19	St. John's, Nfld.
PA	Pacific Coast Command, unallocated	Esquimalt, BC
PD	D Force under COMNORWESTSEAFRON (USN) Pacific coast	Dutch Harbor, Alaska
PE	Esquimalt Force, unallocated, Pacific Coast Command	Esquimalt, BC
PO	Portsmouth Command, unallocated (RN)	Portsmouth, UK
PY	Plymouth Command, unallocated (RN)	Plymouth, UK
QF	Quebec Force, unallocated	Quebec City

RF	Reserve Force (RN) at UK ports as shown in bottom line	various
SM	Sydney Force, based on Mulgrave, NS, as examination vessels	Sydney, NS
SY	Sydney Force, unallocated	Sydney, NS
5-S	5th EG, Newfoundland Command. Mid-ocean support force	St. John's, Nfld.
6-S	6th EG, Newfoundland Command. Mid-ocean support force	St. John's, Nfld.
TA	Training ships, Atlantic Coast Command (later NW Atlantic Command)	Halifax, NS
WA	Western Approaches Command, C.in C., unallocated (RN)	Liverpool, UK
WD	Western Approaches Command, Londonderry, unallocated (RN)	Londonderry
WG	Western Approaches Command, Greenock, unallocated (RN)	Greenock, UK
WL	Western Local Escort Force, unallocated (later Western Escort Force)	Halifax, NS
WS	Western Support Force, Newfoundland Support group for mid-ocean convoys	St. John's, Nfld.
W-1 to W-10	Escort Groups W-1 to W-10, Western Local Escort Force (later Western Escort Force)	St. John's, Nfld.
4-W	4th EG, Western Approaches Command, Greenock (RN)	Greenock, UK
26W	26th EG, Western Mediterranean Fleet (RCN)	Algiers

BOTTOM LINE

Symbol   Status or Location of Ship

FDC	For disposal, Quebec City	N/O	Ship non-operational
FDE	For disposal, Esquimalt, BC	O	Ship operational with Command shown, principally in Canadian waters or North Atlantic, as applicable
FDG	For disposal, Louisburg, NS		
FDH	For disposal, Halifax, NS	OK	Operational, UK waters (includes Gibraltar)
FDJ	For disposal, St. John's, Nfld.	OM	Operational, Mediterranean Sea
FDQ	For disposal, Sorel, PQ	O/P	On passage to another operational area (coast-to-coast or to/from overseas)
FDS	For disposal, Sydney, NS		
F/O	Fitting out, trials, etc. Canadian yards	OSC	Off station in Canadian waters (or acting as local escort in West Atlantic)
FOK	Fitting out, trials, etc., UK yards		
ICL	In reserve, Clyde River, Scotland	OSK	Off station in the UK
IGR	In reserve, Grangemouth, UK	OW	Operational in West Indian waters (includes Caribbean and Bermuda area)
IHA	In reserve, Halifax, NS		
ILO	In reserve, Londonderry, Ireland	RBE	Refitting or repairing, Belfast, Ireland
IMH	In reserve, Milford Haven, Wales	RBO	Refitting or repairing, Boston, MA
		RBT	Refitting or repairing, Baltimore, MD

RCA	Refitting or repairing, Charlottetown, PEI		RMO	Refitting or repairing, Montreal, PQ
RCF	Refitting or repairing, Cardiff, Wales		RNY	Refitting or repairing, New York, NY
RCH	Refitting or repairing, Charleston, SC		RPI	Refitting or repairing, Pictou, NS
RCL	Refitting or repairing, Clyde R., Scotland		RQC	Refitting or repairing, Quebec City, PQ
RCM	Refitting or repairing, Chatham, UK		RSB	Refitting or repairing, Saint John, NB
RDA	Refitting or repairing, Dartmouth, NS		RSC	Refitting or repairing, Scotstoun, Scotland
RES	Refitting or repairing, Esquimalt, BC		RSH	Refitting or repairing, Shelburne, NS
RGA	Refitting or repairing, Galveston, TX		RSN	Refitting or repairing, St. John's, Nfld.
RGR	Refitting or repairing, Greenock, Scotland		RSO	Refitting or repairing, Southampton, UK
RHA	Refitting or repairing, Halifax, NS		RSS	Refitting or repairing, South Shields, UK
RHU	Refitting or repairing, Humber R., UK		RSU	Refitting or repairing, Sunderland, UK
RIC	Refitting or repairing, Hvalfjord, Iceland		RSY	Refitting or repairing, Sydney, NS
RIN	Refitting or repairing, Indiantown, NB		RTY	Refitting or repairing, Tyne River, UK
RLI	Refitting or repairing, Liverpool, NS		RVA	Refitting or repairing, Vancouver, BC
RLN	Refitting or repairing, Londonderry, Ireland		TR	Training duties
RLS	Refitting or repairing, Louisburg, NS		W/U	Working up in Canadian waters
RLU	Refitting or repairing, Lunenburg, NS		WUB	Working up in Bermuda
RLV	Refitting or repairing, Liverpool, UK		WUK	Working up in UK waters

Corvettes

Flower Class, 1939-1940 Programme

NAME of SHIP — Built at / Commissioned

Name / Built at	Commissioned	Nov 40	Dec 40	Jan 41	Feb 41	Mar 41	Apr 41	May 41	June 41	July 41	Aug 41	Sep 41	Oct 41	Nov 41	Dec 41	Jan 42	Feb 42	Mar 42	Apr 42	May 42	June 42	July 42	Aug 42	Sep 42	Oct 42	Nov 42	Dec 42
AGASSIZ — Vancouver	Jan.23/41			PA F/O	PA W/U	PA O/P	HX O	HX O	NF O	19N O	19N O	19N O	N13 O	N13 O	N13 O	NF O	NF RLI	NF RLI	N-2 RHA	A-3 O	A-3 O	A-3 O	C-3 O	C-3 O	C-3 O	C-3 O	C-3 O
ALBERNI — Esquimalt	Feb.4/41				PA W/U	PA O/P	HX O	HX O	NF O	24N O	24N O	24N O	N13 O	NF RHA	NF RHA	NF RHA	N-1 O	N-1 O	N-1 O	N-1 O	NF RHA	NF RHA	NF RHA	NF RHA	26L O/P	26L RLV	26W OM
ALGOMA — Port Arthur	July 11/41									AT F/O	AT W/U	HX O	N14 O	N14 O	N14 O	N14 O	N14 O	N-3 O	A-3 O	A-3 O	NF RLI	WL RLI	WL O	WL O	27L RHA	27L O/P	27L OK
AMHERST — Saint John	Aug.5/41										AT F/O	HX W/U	N16 O	N13 O	N13 O	N11 O	N11 O	N11 O	C-1 O	C-1 O	NF RLI	NF RLI	C-4 O	C-4 O	C-4 O	C-4 O	C-4 O
ARROWHEAD — Sorel	Nov.21/40	AT F/O	AT W/U	AT O/P	WG RSU	WG RSU	WG RSU	WG WUK	4-I O	18N O	18N O	18N O	N12 O	N12 O	NF RCH	NF RCH	N17 O	WL O	WL O	WL O	WL O	GE O	GE O	GE O	GE O	GE O	WL O
ARVIDA — Quebec City	May 22/41							AT F/O	AT W/U	AT W/U	SY O	23N O	N14 WUK	N14 O	N11 O	NF RSB	NF RSB	NF RSB	A-3 O	A-3 O	C-4 O	C-4 O	C-4 O	C-4 O	C-4 O	NF RLU	
BADDECK — Lauzon	May 18/41							AT F/O	AT W/U	HX O	HX RQC	HX OW	N15 RIC	NF RIC	NF RHA	NF RHA	NF RHA	NF RHA	WL W/U	WL O	WL RHA	WL O/P	WL OM	26L 	26W OM		
BARRIE — Collingwood	May 12/41							AT F/O	AT W/U	SY O	SY O	23N O	NF RBE	NF RBE	NF WUK	N12 O	N12 O	N-2 O	N-2 O	N-2 O	WL O	WL O	WL O	WL RLI	WL RLI	WL O	WL O
BATTLEFORD — Collingwood	July 31/41									AT F/O	AT F/O	AT W/U	SY O	SY O	N12 O	NF RLI	NF RLI	NF RLI	C-4 O	C-4 RCF	C-4 RCF	C-1 WUK	C-1 O	C-1 O	C-1 O	C-1 O	
BITTERSWEET — Sorel	Jan.23/41			AT F/O	AT W/U	AT O/P	WG RTY	WG RTY	WG WUK	22N O	22N O	22N O	N11 O	N13 O	N13 O	NF RCH	NF RCH	N-3 O	A-3 O	A-3 O	A-3 O	A-3 O	A-3 O	A-3 O	A-3 RLI	A-3 RLI	
BRANDON — Lauzon	July 22/41									AT F/O	AT F/O	AT W/U	HX O	N15 O	NF RTY	NF RTY	NF RTY	N-1 WUK	C-1 O	C-2 O	C-2 O	C-2 O	C-2 O	C-2 O	C-2 RLI	C-2 RLI	C-4
BUCTOUCHE — Lauzon	June 5/41								AT F/O	AT W/U	21N O	21N O	N12 O	N12 O	N12 O	N12 O	N12 O	N12 O	C-2 O	C-2 O	C-2 O	WL RLU	WL RLU	WL RHA	WL O	WL O	
CAMROSE — Sorel	June 30/41								AT F/O	AT F/O	AT W/U	HX O	N15 O	N15 O	N15 O	N15 O	NF RHA	NF RLU	C-3 RLU	C-3 W/U	C-3 O	WL O	WL O/P	27L OK	27L OK	27L	
CHAMBLY — Montreal	Dec.18/40		AT F/O	AT F/O	HX W/U	HX W/U	HX O	HX O	NF O	21N O	21N O	21N O	N14 O	N14 O	NF RHA	NF RHA	NF RHA	N-2 O	NF OSC	NF OSC	NF OSC	NF OSC	C-1 O	C-1 O	C-1 O	NF RLI	
CHICOUTIMI — Montreal	May 12/41							AT F/O	AT W/U	SY O	SY O	SY O	N14 WUK	N13 O	N13 O	N17 O	N17 O	N18 O	WL RLI	WL RLI	WL O	WL O	WL O	WL O	WL O	WL O	
CHILLIWACK — Vancouver	Apr.8/41						PA F/O	PA W/U	PA O/P	16N OSC	16N O	16N O	N11 O	N11 O	N14 O	NF RHA	N15 O	N-3 O	NF RLI	NF RLI	C-1 O	C-1 O	C-1 O	C-1 O	C-1 O	C-1 O	C-1 O
COBALT — Port Arthur	Nov.25/40	AT F/O	AT F/O	AT F/O	HX W/U	HX W/U	HX O	HX O	NF O	17N O	17N O	17N O	N12 O	N12 O	NF RLI	NF RLI	N12 O	N12 O	C-2 O	C-2 O	WL O	WL O	WL O	WL O	WL O		
COLLINGWOOD — Collingwood	Nov.9/40	AT F/O	AT F/O	HX W/U	HX W/U	HX O	HX O	NF O	25N O	25N O	25N O	N11 O	N11 O	NF RHA	NF RHA	N-1 O	N-1 O	N-1 O	A-3 O	A-3 O	A-3 RLI	A-3 RLI	A-3 RHA	A-3 O	C-4 O		
DAUPHIN — Montreal	May 17/41							AT F/O	AT W/U	SY O	SY O	23N O	N14 WUK	N14 O	N15 O	N15 O	N15 O	N14 O	C-4 O	C-4 O	C-4 O	C-2 RHA	C-2 RHA	C-2 O	C-1 O	C-1 O	A-3
DAWSON — Victoria	Oct.6/41											PA F/O	PA W/U	PA W/U	PA O	PA O	PA O	PA O	PE O	PE O	PE O	PE O	CN O	CN O	PE RES	PE RES	
DRUMHELLER — Collingwood	Sept.13/41											AT F/O	AT W/U	SY O	N14 O	N14 O	N14 O	NF RSO	NF WUK	C-2 O	C-2 O	C-2 O	C-2 O	C-2 O	C-2 O	C-2 RLI	C-2 RLI
DUNVEGAN — Sorel	Sept.9/41											AT F/O	SY W/U	SY O	N16 O	NF RHA	N12 O	N12 O	C-2 O	C-2 O	C-2 O	WL O	WL O	WL O	WL RLI	WL RLI	WL O
EDMUNDSTON — Esquimalt	Oct.21/41												PA F/O	PA W/U	PA W/U	PA O	PA O	PA O	PA O	PE O	PE O	PE O	PE O	PE O/P	WL O	WL O	WL
EYEBRIGHT — Montreal	Nov.26/40	AT F/O	AT W/U	AT O/P	WG RSU	WG RSU	WG RSU	WG WUK	18N O	18N O	18N O	N16 O	N16 O	NF RCH	NF RCH	N14 O	N13 O	C-3 O	C-3 O	C-4 RLV	C-4 RLV	C-1 WUK	C-1 O	C-1 O	C-1 O		
FENNEL — Sorel	Jan.15/41			AT F/O	AT W/U	AT O/P	WG RGR	WG RGR	WG WUK	22N O	22N O	22N O	NF RHA	NF RHA	N11 WUK	N11 O	N11 O	N11 O	C-1 O	C-1 O	WL RNY	WL RNY	WL O	WL O	WL O	WL O	
GALT — Collingwood	May 15/41							AT F/O	AT W/U	21N O	21N O	21N O	N12 O	N15 O	N13 O	N13 O	NF OSC	NF RLI	NF RLI	C-3 W/U	C-3 O	C-3 O	C-3 O	C-3 O	C-3 O		
HEPATICA — Lauzon	Nov.12/40	AT W/U	AT O/P	WG RCL	WG RCL	WG WUK	4-W O	4-W O	4-I O	23N O	23N O	23N O	NF NF	NF RHA	N12 O	N12 O	N12 O	N11 O	N-1 O	N-1 OW	HT OW	HA O	GE O	GE O	HQ O	HQ O	WL O
KAMLOOPS — Victoria	Mar.17/41					PA F/O	PA W/U	PA W/U	HX O/P	HX TR	HX TR	HX TR	HX TR	HX TR	HX TR	HX TR	HX TR	HX TR	HX TR	HX TR	AT TR	AT TR	AT TR	HX TR	AT TR	AT RLI	
KAMSACK — Port Arthur	Oct.4/41												AT F/O	SY W/U	SY O	N13 O	N13 O	N13 O	C-3 O	C-3 O	WL O	WL RHA	WL O	WL O	WL O	WL RLI	WL RLI
KENOGAMI — Port Arthur	June 29/41								AT F/O	AT W/U	24N O	24N O	N16 O	N16 O	N16 O	N17 O	N17 O	WL O	WL O	WL O	WL RHA	WL RHA	WL RHA	WL O	C-1 O	C-1	
LETHBRIDGE — Montreal	June 25/41								AT F/O	AT W/U	SY W/U	N16 O	N16 O	N16 O	N13 O	N14 O	C-4 O	C-4 O	C-4 O	GE O	GE O	WL RLI	WL RLI	ES W/U	O		
LEVIS — Lauzon	May 16/41							AT F/O	AT W/U	HX W/U	19N O	19N O															
LOUISBURG — Quebec City	Oct.2/41												AT F/O	AT W/U	SY O	SY O	NF OSC	N15 O	NF RHA	NF RHA	NF RHA	NF RHA	C-3 O	C-3 O	NF O/P	25L RHU	25L OK	25L RBE
LUNENBURG — Lauzon	Dec.4/41														AT F/O	AT W/U	AT W/U	WL O	WL O	WL O	WL RHA	WL O	HN O	GE O/P	25L OK	25L OM	62G OM
MATAPEDIA — Quebec City	May 9/41							AT F/O	AT W/U	SY O	SY O	SY O	N14 O	N14 O	N13 O	N13 O	N16 O	WL O	WL RPI	WL RPI	WL RPI	WL O	WL O	WL O			
MAYFLOWER — Montreal	Nov.9/40	AT F/O	AT F/O	AT W/U	AT O/P	WG RTY	WG RTY	WG WUK	4-I O	19N O	19N O	19N O	N16 O	N16 O	NF RCH	NF RCH	N-2 O	N-2 O	A-3 O	A-3 O	A-3 O	A-3 O	A-3 RPI	A-3 RPI	A-3		
MONCTON — Saint John	Apr.24/42																		AT F/O	AT W/U	WL O	WL O	WL O	WL O	WL O	WL O	WL O
MOOSE JAW — Collingwood	June 19/41								AT F/O	AT W/U	AT W/U	NF O	NF WUK	N12 O	N12 O	N12 O	N12 O	NF RSB	NF RSB	NF RSB	WL RSB	WL O	WL O	27L RHA	27L O/P	27L OK	
MORDEN — Port Arthur	Sept.6/41											AT F/O	AT W/U	N13 O	NF RGR	NF RSO	NF WUK	N19 O	N19 O	C-2 O	C-2 O	HX O	C-2 O	C-2 RLI	C-2 RLI	C-2 O	C-2 O

	Jan '43	Feb	Mar	Apr	May	June	July	Aug	Sep	Oct	Nov	Dec	Jan '44	Feb	Mar	Apr	May	June	July	Aug	Sep	Oct	Nov	Dec	Jan '45	Feb	Mar	Apr	May	June	July
	NF/RLI	NF/RLI	NF/RLI	C-1/0	C-1/0	C-1/0	C-1/0	C-1/0	C-1/0	C-1/0	C-1/0	C-1/0	C-1/RNY	C-1/RHA	C-1/W/U	C-1/0	W-2/0	W-2/0	W-2/0	W-7/0	W-7/0	W-7/0	W-7/0	W-7/0	W-7/0	W-7/RHA	W-7/RLU	W-7/RLS	W-7/WUB	W-7/0	AT/FDC
	26W/OM	26G/OM	62G/O/P	62L/RHA	WL/0	WL/0	QF/0	QF/0	QF/0	QF/0	QF/RLI	QF/RLI	WL/RLI	WL/WUB	WUB/0	0/O/P	O/P/OK	OK/OK	WG/OK	WG/OK	WG/OK										
	27L/OM	27G/OM	27G/OK	27L/O/P	WS/0	WL/0	QF/0	QF/0	QF/0	QF/0	QF/0	GF/OSK	WL/RLI	WL/RLI	AT/RLI	AT/RHA	C-5/WUB	C-5/0	C-5/0	C-5/0	41H/OK	41H/OK	41H/OK	41H/OK	41H/OK	41H/OK	41H/OK	41M/OK	41H/OK	AT/0	AT/FDS
	C-4/0	C-4/0	C-4/0	C-4/0	C-4/RCA	NF/RCA	C-4/RCA	C-4/RCA	C-4/RCA	C-4/RCA	C-4/W/U	C-4/W/U	C-4/0	C-4/0	C-4/0	C-4/0	C-4/0	C-4/0	C-4/0	C-4/0	C-4/0	C-8/RLI	C-8/RLI	C-8/RLI	HX/WUB	HX/0	C-7/0	HX/0	C-9/0	W-9/0	AT/FDS
	WL/0	WL/0	WL/RCH	WL/RCH	WL/RHA	WL/0	W-7/0	W-7/0	W-7/0	W-7/0	W-7/0	W-1/0	W-1/0	W-1/0	W-1/0	RBT/RBT	RBT/RHA	RHA/WUB	WUB/0	W-1/0	QF/0	QF/RPI	QF/RPI	W-8/0	W-8/0	W-8/0	W-8/RHA	W-8/0	W-8/0	WA/OK	RF/IMH
	NF/RLU	NF/RSB	NF/RHA	A-3/0	C-5/0	C-5/0	C-5/0	C-5/0	C-5/0	C-5/0	C-5/0	C-5/0	C-5/0	C-5/RBT	C-5/RBT	RHA/RHA	W-5/WUB	W-7/0	W-7/0	W-2/0	W-2/0	W-2/0	W-2/0	W-8/0	W-8/0	W-8/0	W-8/RSY	W-8/RSY	W-8/RSY	W-8/OK	AT/FDC
	26W/OM	26G/OM	62G/O/P	62L/RHA	C-4/0	C-4/0	W-2/0	W-2/0	W-2/RLI	W-2/RLI	WL/RLI	WL/RHA	WL/W/U	9-L/OSC	9-L/O/P	9-L/OK	WG/OK	WG/OK	WG/OK	WG/OK	NO/OK	NO/OK	NO/OK	NO/OK	NO/OK	NO/OK	NO/OK	NO/OK	NO/OK	NO/0	AT/FDQ
	WL/0	WL/0	WL/0	WL/0	WL/0	WL/0	W-1/0	W-1/0	W-1/0	W-1/0	W-1/0	W-1/0	W-1/0	W-1/0	W-1/RLI	W-1/RLI	W-1/RHA	W-1/WUB	W-1/0	W-1/0	W-1/0	W-8/0	W-1/0	W-1/0	W-1/0	W-1/0	W-1/0	W-1/0	W-1/0	W-1/0	AT/FDQ
	C-1/0	C-1/0	C-1/0	C-1/0	NF/RLI	NF/0	W-4/RHA	W-4/RHA	W-4/0	W-4/0	W-4/0	W-4/RHA	W-4/0	W-4/0	W-4/RSY	W-3/RSY	W-3/RSY	W-3/RSY	W-3/RHA	W-3/WUB	W-3/0	W-3/0	W-3/0	W-3/0	W-3/0	W-3/0	W-3/0	W-3/0	W-3/0	W-3/0	AT/FDS
	C-3/0	C-3/0	C-3/0	C-3/0	C-3/0	C-3/0	C-3/0	C-3/0	C-3/0	C-3/RBT	C-3/RBT	C-3/W/U	C-3/0	C-3/0	C-3/0	C-3/0	C-3/0	C-3/0	C-3/0	C-3/0	C-3/RPI	C-3/RPI	HX/RHA	HX/RHA	HX/0	HX/0	SY/0	SY/RSY	WA/OK	RF/IGR	
	C-4/0	C-4/0	C-4/0	C-4/0	C-4/0	C-4/0	C-4/0	C-4/RGY	C-4/RGY	C-4/RGY	C-4/0	C-4/W/U	C-4/0	C-4/0	C-4/0	C-4/0	C-4/0	C-4/0	C-4/0	C-4/0	C-6/RLI	C-6/RLI	C-6/RHA	W-7/WUB	W-5/0	W-5/0	W-5/0	W-5/0	W-5/0	W-5/0	AT/FDS
	WL/RHA	WL/0	WL/0	WL/0	WL/0	WL/0	W-1/0	W-1/0	W-1/0	W-1/RSB	W-1/RSB	W-1/RSB	W-1/RSB	WUB/0	0/0	0/0	0/RPI	QF/RPI	QF/RPI	W-1/0	W-1/0	W-1/0	W-1/0	W-1/0	W-1/0	W-1/0	W-1/0	W-1/RSY	W-1/RSY	W-1/0	AT/FDS
	27L/RLN	27G/OM	27G/OM	WL/O/P	WL/RPI	WL/RPI	5-S/RPI	5-S/RPI	5-S/RPI	5-S/RPI	6-S/W/U	6-L/O/P	6-L/OK	6-L/OK	6-L/OK	6-L/OK	WG/OK	WG/OK	WG/OK	WG/OK	PO/O/P	AT/RPI	AT/RPI	AT/WUB	41H/OK	41H/OK	41H/OK	41M/OK	41M/OK	PY/0	AT/FDH
	NF/RLI	NF/O/P	C-2/0	C-2/0	C-2/0	C-2/0	C-2/0	C-2/0	9-S/0	5-S/0	5-S/RLI	5-S/RLI	C-1/RLI	C-1/RLI	C-1/W/U	C-1/0	C-1/0	C-1/0	C-1/0	C-1/0	C-1/0	C-1/0	C-1/0	C-1/0	C-1/0	C-1/0	C-1/0	C-1/RLS	C-1/FDG	C-1/FDQ	
	WL/0	WL/0	WL/0	WL/0	WL/0	WL/RQC	WL/RQC	W-1/RQC	W-1/0	W-1/0	W-1/0	W-1/0	W-1/0	W-1/0	W-1/RLI	W-1/RLI	W-1/RHA	W-3/WUB	W-3/0	W-3/0	TA/TR	TA/TR	TA/TR	TA/TR	TA/TR	TA/TR	RSY/RSY	SY/WUB	SY/0	SY/0	AT/FDC
	C-1/0	A-3/0	NF/RHA	NF/RDA	NF/RDA	C-1/RDA	C-1/RDA	C-1/RDA	C-1/RDA	C-1/W/U	C-1/0	C-1/0	C-1/0	C-1/0	C-1/0	C-1/0	C-1/0	C-1/0	C-1/0	C-1/0	C-1/RSY	C-1/RSY	C-1/RHA	W-8/WUB	W-8/WUB	W-8/0	HX/0	HX/0	HX/0	C-9/0	AT/FDS
	WL/0	WL/0	WL/0	WL/RLI	WL/RLI	WL/RPI	W-6/0	W-6/0	W-6/0	W-6/0	W-6/0	W-6/0	W-6/0	W-6/0	W-6/RLI	W-5/RLI	W-5/RLI	W-5/RLI	W-5/WUB	W-5/0	W-5/0	W-5/0	W-5/0	W-5/0	W-5/0	W-7/0	W-7/0	W-7/0	W-7/0	W-7/0	AT/FDS
	C-4/0	C-4/0	C-4/0	C-4/0	C-4/0	C-4/0	C-4/0	C-4/0	C-4/0	C-4/RNY	C-4/RNY	C-4/W/U	C-4/0	C-4/0	C-4/0	C-4/0	C-4/0	C-4/0	C-4/0	C-4/0	C-4/0	C-7/RLI	C-7/RLI	C-7/RLI	C-7/TR	HX/RHA	HX/TR	HX/FDH	TA/0	TA/0	AT/FDH
	A-3/0	A-3/0	A-3/0	A-3/0	C-5/RPI	C-5/RPI	C-5/RPI	C-5/RPI	C-5/W/U	C-5/0	C-5/0	C-5/0	C-5/0	C-5/0	C-5/0	C-5/0	C-5/0	C-5/0	C-5/0	C-5/RLI	C-5/RLI	C-5/RLI	C-5/WUB	W-7/0	W-7/0	W-7/0	W-7/0	W-7/0	W-7/0	W-7/0	AT/FDQ
	PE/0	PE/0	PD/0	PD/0	PD/0	PD/RES	PE/0	PE/0	PE/0	PE/RVA	PE/RVA	PE/RVA	PE/RVA	PE/0	PE/O/P	AT/0	W-7/0	W-7/0	W-7/0	W-7/0	W-7/0	W-7/0	W-7/0	W-7/0	W-7/0	W-7/RDA	W-7/RDA	W-7/RDA	W-7/0	AT/0	AT/FDQ
	C-2/RLI	C-2/0	C-2/0	C-2/0	C-2/0	C-2/0	C-2/0	C-2/0	C-2/0	C-2/RNY	C-2/RNY	C-2/RNY	C-2/0	C-2/0	C-2/WG	WG/OK	WG/OK	WG/OK	WG/OK	PO/OK	PO/OK	NO/OK	NO/OK	NO/OK	NO/OK	NO/OK	NO/OK	NO/OK	NO/OK	AT/0	AT/FDS
	WL/0	WL/0	WL/0	WL/0	WL/0	WL/0	W-8/0	W-8/0	W-8/0	W-8/RBT	W-8/RBT	W-8/WUB	W-8/0	W-8/0	W-8/0	W-6/0	W-6/0	W-6/0	W-6/0	W-6/0	W-6/0	W-6/0	W-6/0	W-6/RSH	W-6/RSH	W-6/RSH	W-6/WUB	W-6/0	W-6/0	W-6/0	AT/FDQ
	WL/RHA	WL/RHA	WL/RHA	WL/RHA	WL/RHA	WL/W/U	5-S/0	5-S/0	5-S/0	5-S/0	6-S/O/P	6-L/OK	6-L/OK	6-L/OK	6-L/OK	6-L/OK	C-1/O/P	C-1/RLI	C-1/RLI	C-1/WUB	C-8/0	C-8/0	C-8/0	C-8/0	C-8/0	C-8/0	C-8/0	C-8/0	AT/0	AT/0	AT/FDC
	C-3/0	C-3/0	C-3/0	C-3/0	C-3/0	C-3/0	C-3/RBT	C-3/RBT	C-3/W/U	C-3/0	C-3/0	C-3/0	C-3/0	C-3/0	C-3/0	C-3/0	C-3/0	C-3/0	C-3/RPI	C-3/RPI	C-3/WUB	W-3/0	W-3/0	W-3/0	W-3/0	W-3/0	W-3/0	W-3/RHA	WA/RLI	RF/ILO	RF/IMH
	WL/0	WL/0	WL/0	WL/RHA	WL/0	WL/0	C-2/RBT	C-2/RBT	C-2/W/U	C-2/0	C-2/0	C-2/0	C-2/0	C-2/0	C-2/0	C-2/0	C-2/0	C-2/0	C-2/0	C-2/RPI	C-2/RPI	C-2/WUB	C-2/0	C-2/0	C-1/0	C-1/0	C-1/0	C-1/0	RF/ICL	RF/ILO	AT/FDQ
	NF/RLI	NF/RLI	NF/RHA	NF/W/U	C-1/0	C-1/0	C-1/0	C-1/0	C-1/0	C-1/0	C-1/0	C-1/0	C-1/0	C-1/0	C-1/RNY	C-1/RNY	W-5/RHA	W-5/WUB	W-5/0	W-5/0	W-5/0	W-5/0	W-5/0	W-5/0	W-5/0	W-5/0	W-5/0	W-5/0	W-5/WA	W-5/OK	AT/IMH
	WL/0	WL/RNY	WL/RNY	WL/RHA	WL/0	WL/0	W-5/0	W-5/0	W-5/0	W-5/0	W-5/0	W-5/0	W-5/0	W-5/0	W-4/RNY	W-4/RNY	W-4/RHA	W-4/WUB	W-4/0	W-4/0	W-4/0	W-4/0	W-4/0	W-4/0	W-4/0	W-4/0	W-4/0	W-4/RHA	WA/RLI	RF/OK	RF/IMH
	AT/RLI	AT/RLI	WL/W/U	WL/0	WL/0	C-2/0	C-2/0	C-2/0	C-2/0	C-2/0	C-2/0	C-2/0	C-2/RCA	C-2/RCA	C-2/RCA	C-2/W/U	C-2/WUB	C-2/0	C-2/0	C-2/0	C-2/0	C-2/0	C-2/0	C-2/0	C-2/0	C-2/0	C-2/0	C-2/0	HX/0	AT/0	AT/FDQ
	WL/RHA	WL/0	WL/0	WL/0	WL/0	WL/0	W-4/RBT	W-4/RBT	W-4/W/U	W-4/0	W-4/0	W-4/0	W-4/RBT	W-3/RBT	W-3/W/U	W-3/0	W-3/0	W-3/0	W-3/0	W-3/0	W-3/0	W-3/0	W-3/0	W-3/0	W-3/0	W-3/0	W-3/RHA	W-3/RLI	W-3/RLI	W-3/WUB	AT/FDH
	C-1/0	C-1/0	C-1/0	C-1/0	C-1/RLI	NF/RLI	W-8/0	W-8/0	W-8/0	W-8/0	W-8/0	W-8/0	W-8/0	W-8/0	W-8/0	W-8/0	W-6/RLI	W-6/RLI	W-6/RLI	W-6/W/U	W-6/WUB	W-6/0	W-6/0	W-8/0	W-8/0	W-8/0	W-8/0	W-8/0	W-8/0	W-8/0	AT/FDS
	ES/0	ES/0	ES/0	WL/WL	WL/0	WL/0	W-3/W-3	W-3/0	W-3/0	W-3/0	W-3/0	W-3/0	W-3/RSY	W-3/RSY	W-3/RHA	W-5/WUB	W-5/RPI	W-5/0	W-5/0	W-5/0	W-5/0	W-5/0	W-5/0	W-5/0	W-5/0	W-5/RSH	W-5/RSH	W-5/T	W-5/FDH		
	25L/RBE	25G/OM																													
	62G/OM	62G/OM	62G/OK	62L/RLV	WL/RLV	WL/RLV	5-S/RLV	5-S/0	5-S/0	5-S/0	6-S/O/P	6-L/OK	6-L/OK	6-L/OK	6-L/OK	6-G/OK	6-G/OK	6-G/OK	6-G/CK	41H/OK	AT/RSB	AT/RSB	AT/RSB	AT/WUB	NO/OK	NO/OK	NO/OK	41M/OK	41M/OK	PY/OK	AT/FDH
	WL/0	WL/0	WL/0	WL/0	WL/0	WL/0	W-5/0	W-5/0	W-5/0	W-5/RDA	W-5/RLI	W-5/RLI	W-5/RLI	W-5/RHA	W-4/WUB	W-4/0	W-4/0	W-4/0	W-4/0	W-4/0	W-4/0	W-4/0	W-4/0	W-4/RHA	GF/RLI	GF/RHA	W-4/WUB	W-4/FDC	W-4/FDC	AT/0	AT/FDC
	A-3/W/U	C-3/0	C-3/0	C-3/0	C-3/0	C-3/0	C-3/RBT	C-3/RBT	C-3/W/U	C-3/WUB	C-3/0	C-3/0	C-3/0	C-3/WG	WG/OK	WG/OK	WD/OK	WD/OK	PO/OK	PO/OK	PO/OK	PO/OK	PO/OK	PO/OK	PO/OK	PO/OK	PO/OK	PO/IGR	RF/IGR		
	WL/0	WL/0	WL/0	WL/0	WL/0	WL/0	W-5/0	W-5/RDA	W-5/RDA	W-5/RDA	W-5/0	PE/O/P	PE/0	PE/0	PE/0	PE/0	PE/RVA	PE/RVA	PE/0	PE/0	PE/0	PE/0	PE/0	PE/0	PE/0	PE/0	PE/0	PE/0	PE/0	PE/0	PA/0
	27L/OK	27G/OM	27G/OM	WL/O/P	WL/RHA	QF/0	QF/0	QF/0	QF/0	QF/0	GF/0	GF/0	WL/RLI	WL/RLI	AT/W/U	AT/O/P	WD/OK	WG/OK	WG/OK	41H/OK	41H/OK	41H/OK	41H/OK	41H/OK	41H/OK	41H/OK	41M/OK	41M/OK	AT/0	AT/FDS	
	C-2/0	C-2/0	C-2/0	C-2/0	C-2/0	C-2/0	C-2/RLU	C-2/RLU	9-M/W/U	C-2/0	C-2/0	C-2/RLN	C-2/RLN	C-2/0	C-2/0	C-2/0	C-2/0	C-2/0	C-2/0	C-2/0	C-2/0	C-2/0	C-2/0	HX/RSY	HX/RSY	HX/RHA	HX/WUB	W-9/0	W-9/0	AT/FDS	

Flower Class, 1939-1940 Programme continued

NAME of SHIP / Built at	Commissioned	Nov '40	Dec	Jan '41	Feb	Mar	Apr	May	Jun	Jul	Aug	Sep	Oct	Nov '41	Dec	Jan '42	Feb	Mar	Apr	May	Jun	Jul	Aug	Sep	Oct	Nov	Dec
NANAIMO / Esquimalt	Apr.26/41						PA/F/O	PA/W/U	HX/O/P	HX/O	HX/RHA	NF/RHA	N16/O	N16/O	N13/O	N13/O	N16/O	WL/O	WL/O	WL/O	WL/O	WL/RHA	WL/RHA	WL/O	WL/O	WL/O	WL/O
NAPANEE / Kingston	May 12/41							AT/F/O	AT/F/O	SY/W/U	SY/O	SY/O	N14/O	N14/O	N14/O	N13/O	N13/O	N12/O	C-2/O	C-2/O	NF/O	NF/RLI	NF/W/U	C-1/O	C-1/O	C-1/O	C-1/O
OAKVILLE / Port Arthur	Nov.18/41													AT/F/O	AT/W/U	WL/O	WL/O	WL/O	WL/O	WL/O	HA/OW	HA/OW	ES/O	ES/RHA	ES/RHA	ES/O	
ORILLIA / Collingwood	Nov.25/40	AT/F/O	AT/F/O	AT/F/O	HX/W/U	HX/W/U	HX/O	HX/O	NF/O	24N/O	24N/O	24N/O	N14/O	N14/O	N13/O	NF/RHA	NF/RHA	NF/RHA	C-1/O	C-1/O	C-1/O	C-1/O	C-1/O	C-1/O	C-2/O	C-2/O	
PICTOU / Lauzon	Apr.29/41							AT/F/O	AT/W/U	NF/O	21N/O	21N/O	21N/O	N11/O	N14/O	N12/O	NF/RHA	NF/RSN	N16/O	NF/RLV	NF/RLV	C-4/O	C-4/Ø	C-4/N/O	C-2/RHA	C-2/O	C-2/O
PRESCOTT / Kingston	June 26/41							AT/F/O	AT/F/O	HX/W/U	23N/O	N16/O	N16/O	N16/O	N11/O	NF/RLI	C-4/RLI	C-4/O	C-4/O	WL/O	WL/O	WL/O	WL/0/P	25L/RHU	25L/OK	25L/OK	
QUESNEL / Victoria	May 23/41							PA/F/O	PA/W/U	PA/O	PA/O	PA/O	PA/O	PA/O	PA/O	PA/O	PA/O	PA/O	PA/O	PE/O	PE/O	PE/O	PE/RES	PE/O	WL/0/P	WL/O	WL/O
RIMOUSKI / Lauzon	Apr.26/41							AT/F/O	AT/W/U	NF/O	16N/O	16N/O	16N/O	NF/RHA	NF/RHA	NF/RHA	N13/O	N13/O	N13/O	C-3/O	C-3/O	WL/O	WL/O	WL/O	WL/O	WL/O	WL/O
ROSTHERN / Port Arthur	June 17/41								AT/F/O	AT/W/U	HX/O	HX/O	N15/O	NF/WUK	N11/O	NF/RHA	NF/RHA	N-2/O	N-2/O	A-3/O	A-3/O	A-3/RLI	WL/O	A-3/O	A-3/O	A-3/O	A-3/O
SACKVILLE / Saint John	Dec.30/41														AT/F/O	AT/F/O	AT/W/U	WL/O	WL/RHA	C-3/O	C-3/O	C-3/O	C-3/O	C-3/O	C-3/O	C-3/O	C-3/O
SASKATOON / Montreal	June 9/41								AT/F/O	AT/W/U	HX/OW	HX/OW	HX/O	HX/RHA	HX/O	HX/O	WL/O	WL/O	WL/O	WL/O	WL/O	WL/RHA	WL/RHA	WL/RHA	WL/RHA	WL/O	WL
SHAWINIGAN / Lauzon	Sept.19/41											AT/F/O	AT/W/U	SY/O	SY/O	N14/O	N14/O	N14/O	C-4/O	C-4/O	C-4/O	HN/O	HN/O	HN/O	HQ/O	HQ/O	WL/RLI
SHEDIAC / Lauzon	July 8/41									AT/F/O	AT/W/U	SY/O	N15/O	N15/O	N15/O	N15/O	N-3/O	A-3/O	A-3/O	WL/RLI	WL/RLI	WL/O	WL/O	C-1/O	C-1/O		
SHERBROOKE / Sorel	June 5/41								AT/F/O	AT/W/U	HX/O	SY/O	N14/WUK	N-1/O	N11/O	N12/O	N12/O	N13/O	C-3/RLU	NF/RLU	NF/O	C-4/O	C-4/O	C-4/O	C-4/O	C-4/O	
SNOWBERRY / Lauzon	Nov.30/40	AT/F/O	AT/F/O	AT/W/U	AT/O/P	WG/RCL	WG/WUK	WG/O	4-I/O	15N/O	15N/O	15N/O	N11/O	N11/O	NF/RCH	NF/RCH	WL/O	WL/O	WL/O	HT/OW	HA/OW	HA/OW	ES/O	ES/O	ES/O	ES/O	
SOREL / Sorel	Aug.19/41									AT/F/O	AT/W/U	SY/O	SY/O	N13/O	N17/O	NF/RLE	NF/RLE	N11/WUK	NF/OSC	WL/O	WL/O	WL/O	WL/O	WL/O	WL/O	WL/RLI	WL/RLI
SPIKENARD / Lauzon	Dec.8/40		AT/F/O	AT/O/P	WG/RSS	WG/RSS	WG/WUK	WG/O	4-I/O	16N/O	16N/O	16N/O	N11/RHA	NF/RLI	NF/O	N15/O	N15/O										
SUDBURY / Kingston	Oct.15/41											AT/F/O	AT/W/U	SY/O	SY/O	N16/O	WL/O	WL/O	WL/O	HT/OW	HT/OW	HA/OW	HA/O	ES/O	ES/O	ES/O	ES/O
SUMMERSIDE / Quebec City	Sept.11/41											AT/F/O	AT/W/U	SY/O	N14/O	N14/O	N14/O	N18/O	WL/O	WL/O	WL/O	GE/O	GE/O	GE/O	26L/0/P	26L/OK	26W/OM
THE PAS / Collingwood	Oct.21/41												AT/F/O	AT/W/U	HX/O	HX/O	HX/O	WL/O	WL/O	HT/OW	HT/OW	HA/OW	HA/O	ES/O	ES/O	ES/O	WL/RLI
TRAIL / Vancouver	Apr.30/41						PA/F/O	PA/W/U	HX/O	17N/O	17N/O	17N/O	N11/O	N11/O	N11/O	N13/O	N12/O	N12/O	C-2/O	C-2/O	HX/O	HN/O	HN/O	HN/O	HQ/O	HQ/O	WL/O
TRILLIUM / Montreal	Oct.31/40	AT/F/O	AT/O/P	WG/RGR	WG/RGR	WG/WUK	4-W/O	4-W/O	4-I/O	18N/O	23N/O	NF/RLU	NF/RHA	NF/RHA	N14/O	N13/O	N13/O	N13/O	C-3/RGA	NF/RGA	NF/RGA	NF/W/U	A-3/O	A-3/O	A-3/O	A-3/O	
WETASKIWIN / Vancouver	Dec.17/40		PA/F/O	PA/W/U	PA/W/U	PA/O/P	HX/O	HX/O	NF/O	20N/O	20N/RHA	20N/O	N15/O	N15/O	N15/O	NF/RLI	C-3/RLI	C-3/RLI	C-3/W/U	C-3/O	C-3/O	C-3/O	C-3/O	C-3/O	C-3/O		
WEYBURN / Port Arthur	Nov.26/41													AT/F/O	AT/W/U	AT/W/U	AT/O	WL/RHA	WL/O	WL/O	WL/O	GE/O	GE/O	GE/0/P	25L/RLV	62G/OM	62G/OM
WINDFLOWER / Lauzon	Oct.20/40	AT/F/O	AT/O/P	WG/RSC	WG/RSC	WG/WUK	4-W/O	4-W/O	4-I/O	18N/O	23N/O	NF/RLI	NF/RLI	N12/O	N12/O												

Flower Class, 1940-1941 Programme

NAME of SHIP / Built at	Commissioned	Nov '41	Dec	Jan '42	Feb	Mar	Apr	May	Jun	Jul	Aug	Sep	Oct	Nov '42	Dec	Jan '43	Feb	Mar	Apr	May	Jun	Jul	Aug	Sep	Oct	Nov	Dec
BRANTFORD / Midland	May 15/42							AT/F/O	AT/W/U	WL/O	WL/O	WL/O	WL/O	WL/O	WL/O	WL/O	WL/O	WL/O	WL/O	WL/O	W-3/RQC	W-3/RQC	W-3/W/U	W-3/O	W-3/O	W-3/O	
CALGARY / Sorel	Dec.16/41		AT/F/O	AT/W/U	AT/O	WL/O	WL/O	WL/O	WL/O	WL/O	WL/O	WL/O	WL/0/P	WL/OK	27L/OK	27L/RCF	27L/RCF	27L/RCF	27G/0/P	WL/RHA	WL/O	5-S/O	5-S/O	5-S/O	5-S/O	6-S/0/P	6-L/O
CHARLOTTETOWN / Kingston	Dec.13/41		AT/F/O	AT/W/U	AT/O	WL/O	WL/O	WL/O	WL/O	GE	GE	GE															
DUNDAS / Victoria	Apr.1/42						PA/F/O	PE/W/U	PE/O	PE/O	PE/O	PE/0/P	WL/O	WL/O	WL/O	WL/O	WL/O	WL/O	WL/O	WL/O	W-7/RMO	W-7/RMO	W-7/RMO	W-7/RMO	W-7/RMO	W-5/RMO	
FREDERICTON / Sorel	Dec.8/41		AT/F/O	AT/W/U	AT/O	WL/O	WL/O	WL/RHA	HA/O	HA/OW	ES/OW	ES/O	ES/O	ES/O	ES/O	ES/O	WL/O	WL/O	C-1/RLI	C-1/RLI	C-1/RLI	C-1/RLI	C-1/W/U	C-1/O			
HALIFAX / Collingwood	Nov.26/41	AT/0/P	AT/F/O	AT/W/U	AT/O	WL/O	WL/O	WL/O	WL/O	HA/HA	HA/O	ES/O	ES/O	ES/O	ES/O	ES/O	ES/O	WL/O	WL/O	WL/RLI	C-3/RLI	C-3/RLI	C-3/RLI	C-3/RLI	C-3/W/U	C-3/RHA	
KITCHENER / Lauzon	June 28/42								AT/0/P	AT/F/O	AT/W/U	WL/O	27L/0/P	27L/RLV	27L/OK	27L/OK	27L/OM	27G/OM	WL/0/P	WS/O	5-S/O	5-S/O	C-5/O	C-5/RLI	C-5/RLI	C-5	C-5
La MALBAIE / Sorel	Apr.28/42							AT/F/O	AT/W/U	AT/O	WL/O	WL/RHA	WL/RHA	WL/RHA	NF/RHA	NF/O	C-3/O	C-3/O	C-3/O	C-3/O	C-3/O	C-3/O	C-3/O	C-3/RLI	C-3/RLI	C-3/RLI	
MIDLAND / Midland	Nov.17/41	AT/F/O	AT/W/U	AT/O	AT/O	WL/O	WL/O	WL/O	WL/O	WL/O	WL/O	WL/O	WL/O	WL/O	WL/RLI	WL/RLI	WL/RHA	WL/RHA	WL/RHA	W-2/O	W-2/O	W-2/O	W-2/O	W-2/O	W-2/O		
NEW WESTMINSTER / Victoria	Jan.31/42			PA/F/O	PA/F/O	PA/W/U	PA/O	PE/O	PE/O	PE/O	PE/0/P	PE/RHA	WL/O	WL/O	WL/O	WL/O	WL/O	WL/O	WL/O	WL/RSY	C-5/RSY	C-5/RSY	C-5/RSY	C-5/RSY	C-5/RSY	C-5/RSY	C-5/RHA
PORT ARTHUR / Port Arthur	May 26/42							AT/F/O	AT/W/U	AT/O	WL/O	WL/0/P	26L/OK	26L/OM	26L/OM	26W/OM	26G/OM	62G/0/P	WL/O	WS/O	5-S/O	W-9/RLI	W-9/RLI	W-9/RLI	W-9/RLI	W-9/RHA	

```
1943                                                    1944                                                    1945
Jan. Feb. Mar. Apr. May June July Aug. Sep. Oct. Nov. Dec.  Jan. Feb. Mar. Apr. May June July Aug. Sep. Oct. Nov. Dec.  Jan. Feb. Mar. Apr. May June July

WL   WL   WL   WL   WL   WL   W-9  W-9  W-9  W-9  W-9  W-9   W-9  W-9  W-9  W-9  W-7  W-7  W-7  W-7  W-7  W-7  W-7  W-7   PA   PA   PA   PA   PA   PA   PA   PA
0    0    0    0    0    0    0    0    0    RLU  RLU  0     0    0    0    0    0    0    0    0    0    0    0    0/P   0    RES  RES  RES  TR   TR   TR   0

C-1  C-1  C-1  C-1  C-1  NF   C-1  C-3  C-3  C-3  C-3  C-3   C-3  C-3  C-3  C-3  C-3  C-3  C-3  C-3  C-3  C-4  C-4  W-2   W-2  W-2  W-2  W-2  W-2  W-2  W-2  AT
0    0    0    0    0    RMO  RMO  RMO  RMO  RMO  RHA  W/U   0    0    0    0    0    0    0    0    0    0    0    RPI   RPI  RHA  WUB  0    0    0    0    FDS

ES   ES   ES   WL   WL   WL   W-7  W-7  W-7  W-7  W-7  W-7   W-8  W-8  W-8  W-8  W-8  W-6  W-6  W-6  W-6  W-6  W-6  W-6   W-6  W-6  W-6  W-6  W-6  RLU  RLU  RLU  FDS
0    0    0    0    0    0    0    0    0    0    0    0     RGA  RGA  RGA  RHA  WUB  0    0    0    0    0    0    0     0    0    0    0    0

C-2  NF   NF   NF   C-4  C-4  C-4  C-4  C-4  C-4  C-4  C-4   C-4  C-4  C-4  C-4  C-4  W-2  W-2  W-2  W-2  W-2  W-2  W-2   W-2  W-2  W-2  W-2  W-2  RSN  N/O  FDS
0    RLI  RLI  RLI  0    0    0    0    0    0    0    0     RLI  RLI  RLI  RLI  RHA  WUB  0    0    0    0    0    0     0    0    0    0    0

NF   NF   NF   NF   C-3  C-3  C-3  C-3  C-3  C-3  C-3  C-3   C-3  C-3  C-3  C-3  W-5  W-5  W-5  W-5  W-5  W-5  W-5  W-5   W-5  W-5  W-5  W-5  W-5  AT
RHA  RLI  RLI  RHA  RNY  RNY  RNY  0    0    0    0    0     RNY  RNY  0    WUB  0    0    0    0    0    0    0    0     0    0    0    0    0    FDQ

27L  27G  27G  WL   WL   WL   5-S  5-S  5-S  5-S  6-S  6-L   6-L  6-L  6-L  6-L  WG   WG   WG   WG   PO   PO   AT   AT    AT   AT   AT   PO   NO   NO   AT   AT
OK   OM   O/P  RHA  RLI  RLI  RLI  RLI  RLI  RLI  W/U  O/P   OK   OK   OK   OK   OK   OK   OK   OK   OK   O/P  RLI  RLI   RLI  WUB  OK   OK   OK   0    FDH

WL   WL   WL   WL   WL   WL   W-1  W-1  W-1  W-1  W-1  W-1   W-1  W-1  W-1  W-1  QF   QF   QF   QF   QF   HX   HX   HX    HX   HX   HX   HX   HX   AT
0    0    0    0    0    0    0    0    0    RPI  RPI  RPI   RHA  WUB  0    0    0    0    0    0    0    0    0    RSY   RSY  WUB  0    0    0    0    FDQ

WL   WL   WL   WL   WL   WL   C-1  C-1  C-1  C-1  C-1  C-1   C-3  C-3  C-3  C-3  WG   WG   WG   WG   AT   TA   AT   AT    AT   AT   AT   41H  41H  PY   AT
0    0    0    RLI  RLI  RLI  RLI  RLI  W/U  0    0    0     0    0    0    OK   OK   OK   OK   OK   O/P  TR   RLS  RLS   RLI  WUB  OK   OK   OK   OK   FDH

A-3  A-3  A-3  A-3  C-5  C-5  C-5  C-5  C-5  C-5  C-5  C-5   C-5  C-5  C-5  C-5  C-5  TA   TA   TA   TA   TA   HX   HX    HX   HX   HX   HX   HX   AT
0    0    0    0    0    0    RSH  RSH  RSH  W/U  0    0     0    0    0    0    TR   TR   TR   TR   TR   WUB  0    0     0    0    0    0    0    FDS

NF   NF   NF   NF   C-1  C-1  C-1  C-1  TA   C-2  C-2  C-2   C-2  C-2  C-2  C-2  C-2  C-2  C-2  C-2  TA   TA   AT   AT    AT   AT   AT   AT   AT   AT   AT
0    RLI  RLI  RLI  0    0    0    0    0    0    0    0     RGA  RHA  WUB  0    0    0    TR   TR   RDA  RDA  RDA  RDA   RDA  RHA  RHA  RHA  RHA

WL   WL   WL   WL   WL   WL   W-8  W-8  W-8  W-8  W-8  W-8   W-8  W-8  W-8  W-8  W-6  W-6  W-6  W-6  W-6  W-6  W-6  W-6   W-6  W-6  W-6  W-6  W-6  W-6  W-6  AT
0    0    0    0    0    0    0    0    0    0    0    0     RPI  RPI  RPI  RPI  WUB  0    0    0    0    0    0    0     0    0    0    0    0    0    0    FDS

WL   WL   WL   WL   WL   WL   W-3  W-3  W-3  W-3  W-3  W-3   W-3  W-3  W-3  W-2  W-2  W-2  W-2  W-8  W-2
RLI  RHA  RHA  0    0    0    0    0    0    0    0    0     0    RHA  RLI  RHA  WUB  RSH  0    0    0

C-1  C-1  C-1  C-1  NF   NF   W-8  W-8  W-8  W-8  W-8  W-8   W-8  W-8  PE   PE   PE   PE   PE   PE   PE   PE   PE   PE    PE   PE   PE   PE   PE   PE   PE   PA
0    0    0    0    RLI  RLI  0    0    0    0    0    0     0    0    O/P  0    RVA  RVA  0    0    0    0    0    0     0    0    0    0    0    0    0    0

C-4  C-4  C-4  A-3  NF   NF   W-2  W-2  W-2  W-2  W-2  W-2   W-2  W-2  W-2  W-2  W-7  W-7  W-7  W-7  W-7  W-7  W-1  W-1   W-1  W-1  W-1  W-1  W-1  W-1  W-1  AT
0    0    0    0    RLU  RLU  0    0    0    0    0    0     0    0    0    RLI  RLI  RHA  WUB  0    0    0    0    0     0    0    0    0    0    0    0    FDS

ES   ES   ES   WL   WL   WL   5-S  5-S  5-S  5-S  6-S  6-L   6-L  6-L  6-L  W-6  W-6  W-6  AT   AT   PO   PO   PO   PO    PO   PO   PO   PO   PO   RF   RF
0    0    0    RCH  RCH  0    0    0    0    0    0    O/P   OK   OK   RBT  RBT  RHA  WUB  0    O/P  OK   OK   OK   OK    OK   OK   OK   OK   OK   IGR  IGR

WL   TA   TA   TA   TA   TA   TA   TA   C-5  C-5  WL   WL    WL   AT   AT   W-4  W-4  W-4  W-4  W-4  W-4  W-4  W-4  W-4   W-4  W-4  W-4  W-4  W-4  W-4  W-4  AT
RPI  TR   TR   TR   TR   TR   TR   TR   0    0    RHA  RHA   RDA  RDA  RDA  WUB  0    0    RBB  0    0    0    0    0     RHA  0    0    0    RSY  RSY  FDS


ES   ES   WL   WL   WL   WL   W-9  W-9  W-9  W-9  W-9  W-9   W-9  PE   PE   PE   PE   PE   PE   PE   PE   PE   PE   PE    PE   PE   PE   PE   PE   PA
RLI  RLI  0    0    0    0    0    0    0    OSK  0    0     0/P  RVA  RVA  RVA  W/U  0    0    0    0    0    0    0     0    0    0    0    RES  RES  0    0

26W  26G  62G  WL   WL   WL   QF   QF   QF   QF   NF   C-5   C-5  C-5  C-5  C-5  WG   WG   WG   WG   41H  AT   AT   AT    AT   AT   PO   PO   PO   AT   AT
OM   OM   O/P  RSB  RSB  RSB  RSB  RSB  RSB  W/U  0    0     0    0    0    0    OK   OK   OK   OK   OK   O/P  RLI  RLI   RHA  WUB  O/P  OK   OK   0    FDS

WL   WL   WL   WL   WL   WL   W-4  W-4  W-4  W-4  W-4  W-4   W-4  W-4  W-4  W-4  W-3  W-3  W-3  W-3  W-8  AT   TA   TA    TA   TA   TA   TA   TA   AT
RLI  0    0    0    0    0    0    RSH  RSH  W/U  0    0     0    0    0    0    0    0    0    0    RLI  RSY  RSY  TR    TR   TR   TR   TR   TR   FDH

WL   WL   WL   WL   WL   WL   W-6  W-6  W-6  W-6  W-6  W-6   W-6  W-6  W-6  W-5  W-5  W-5  W-5  W-5  W-5  W-5  W-4  W-4   W-4  W-4  W-4  W-4  W-4  AT
0    0    0    0    0    0    RLU  RLU  RHA  W/U  0    0     0    0    0    0    0    0    RLI  RLI  RLI  RHA  WUB  0     0    0    0    0    0    FDS

A-3  A-3  A-3  A-3  A-3  C-4  C-4  C-4  C-4  C-4  C-4  C-4   C-4  C-4  C-4  C-3  C-3  C-3  C-3  C-3  C-3  C-3  C-3  C-3   C-3  C-3  C-3  C-3  AT   WA   RF
0    0    0    0    RBO  RBO  W/U  0    0    0    0    0     0    0    0    RPI  RPI  RHA  WUB  0    0    0    0    0     0    0    0    0    OK   IMH

NF   NF   NF   A-3  C-5  C-5  C-5  C-5  C-5  C-5  C-5  C-5   C-5  C-5  C-5  C-5  C-5  C-5  C-5  W-7  W-7  W-7  W-7  W-7   W-7  W-7  AT
RLI  RLI  RHA  0    0    0    0    0    0    0    0    RGA   RGA  RGA  RHA  WUB  0    0    0    0    0    0    0    0     0    0    FDQ

62G  62G
OM   OM
```

```
1944                                                    1945
Jan. Feb. Mar. Apr. May June July Aug. Sep. Oct. Nov.  Dec.  Jan. Feb. Mar. Apr. May June July

W-3  W-3  W-3  W-3  W-2  C-3  W-2  W-2  W-2  TA   TA    TA   TA   TA   TA   TA   TA   TA   AT
0    0    0    0    0    0    0    0    RSY  RSY  TR    TR   TR   TR   TR   TR   TR   TR   TR

6-L  6-L  6-L  6-L  WD   WG   WG   WG   NO   NO   NO    NO   NO   NO   NO   NO   NO   AT   AT
RLI  RLI  RLI  W/U  OK   OK   OK   OK   OK   OK   OK    OK   OK   OK   OK   OK   OK   0    FDC


W-5  W-5  W-5  W-5  W-4  W-4  W-4  W-4  W-4  W-4  W-4   W-4  W-4  W-4  W-4  W-4  W-4  W-4  AT
W/U  0    0    0    0    0    0    0    0    0    0     0    RLI  RLI  WUB  0    0    0    FDS

C-1  C-1  C-1  C-1  C-1  C-1  C-1  C-1  C-1  C-1  C-7   C-7  C-7  HX   C-9  C-9  C-9  C-9  AT
0    0    0    0    0    0    0    0    0    0    RSB   RSB  WUB  0    0    0    0    0    FDS

C-1  C-1  C-1  C-1  C-1  C-1  C-1  C-1  C-1  C-1  C-1   C-1  HX   C-9  C-9  C-9  C-9  C-9  AT
0    0    0    0    0    0    0    0    RLU  RLU  RLU   RHA  WUB  0    0    0    0    0    FDS

C-5  C-5  C-5  C-5  WG   WG   WG   WG   41H  41H  41H   41H  41H  41H  41H  41M  41H  AT   AT
RLI  WUB  0    0    OK   OK   OK   OK   OK   OK   OK    OK   OK   OK   OK   OK   OK   0    FDS

C-3  C-3  C-3  C-3  C-3  C-3  C-3  C-3  C-3  C-3  C-3   C-3  HX   HX   HX   HX   W-9  W-9  AT
W/U  0    0    0    0    0    0    0    0    0    0     0    RLS  0    WUB  0    0    0    FDQ

W-2  W-2  W-2  W-2  W-2  W-2  W-2  W-2  W-2  W-2  W-2   W-2  W-2  W-2  W-2  W-2  W-2  AT
0    0    RGA  RGA  RGA  RHA  WUB  0    0    0    0     0    0    0    0    0    0    FDS

C-5  C-5  C-5  C-5  C-5  C-5  C-5  C-5  C-5  C-5  C-5   C-5  HX   HX   HX   SY   SY   AT
W/U  0    0    0    0    0    0    0    0    0    0     0    RSB  RSB  RSB  WUB  0    FDS  FDQ

W-9  W-9  W-9  W-9  WD   WG   WD   WD   WD   PO   PO    PO   PO   PO   PO   AT   AT   AT   AT
W/U  0    0    0    OK   OK   OK   OK   OK   OK   OK    OK   OK   OK   O/P  RLI  RLI  RLI  FDS
```

167

Flower Class, 1940-1941 Programme, Continued

Year columns: first 2 months = 1941 (Nov–Dec); next 12 = 1942 (Jan–Dec); last 12 = 1943 (Jan–Dec). Each ship has two data lines.

NAME of SHIP / Built at / Commissioned	Nov	Dec	Jan	Feb	Mar	Apr	May	Jun	Jul	Aug	Sep	Oct	Nov	Dec	Jan	Feb	Mar	Apr	May	Jun	Jul	Aug	Sep	Oct	Nov	Dec
REGINA — Sorel — Jan.22/42			AT	AT	WL	WL	WL	WL	WL	WL	WL	WL	27L	27L	27L	27L	27G	WL	WL	WL	QF	QF	QF	QF	NF	NF
			F/O	W/U	O	O	O	O	O	O	O	RHA	O/P	RBE	OK	OM	O/P	O	O	RSY	RSY	RSY	RSY	RPI	RPI	RPI
TIMMINS — Esquimalt — Feb.10/42				PA	PA	PA	PE	PE	PE	PE	PE	PE	WL	WL	WL	WL	WL	WL	WL	WL	W-6	W-6	W-6	W-6	W-6	W-6
				F/O	W/U	O	O	O	O	O	O	O/P	O	O	O	O	O	O	O	O	O	RLI	RLI	W/U	O	O
VANCOUVER — Esquimalt — Mar.20/42					PA	PA	PE	PE	PE	PE	CN	CN	PE	PE	PE	PE	PD	PD	PD	PD	PE	PE	PE	PE	PE	PE
					F/O	W/U	O	O	O	O	O	O	O	O	O	O	O	O	O	O	RVA	RVA	RVA	RVA	O	O
VILLE de QUEBEC — Quebec City — May 24/42							AT	AT	AT	WL	WL	WL	26L	26L	26W	26G	62G	WL	QF	QF	QF	QF	WL	W-2	W-2	W-2
							F/O	W/U	O	O	O	O	RLV	OM	OM	RGI	RGI	O/P	O	O	O	O	O	O	O	O
WOODSTOCK — Collingwood — May 1/42								AT	AT	WL	WL	WL	25L	25L	25L	25L	25L	27G	C-1	C-1	5-S	C-4	C-4	C-4	C-4	C-4
								F/O	W/U	O	O	O/P	RHU	OK	OK	OK	OM	O/P	O	O	O	RLI	RLI	W/U	O	O

Revised Flower Class (I.E.), 1942-1943 Programme

Year columns: first 3 months = 1943 (Oct–Dec); next 12 = 1944 (Jan–Dec); last 7 = 1945 (Jan–Jul). Each ship has two data lines.

NAME of SHIP / Built at / Commissioned	Oct	Nov	Dec	Jan	Feb	Mar	Apr	May	Jun	Jul	Aug	Sep	Oct	Nov	Dec	Jan	Feb	Mar	Apr	May	Jun	Jul
ATHOLL — Quebec City — Oct.14/43	NC	NC	NC	NC	9-L	9-L	9-L	C-4	C-4	C-4	C-4	C-4	C-4	C-4	C-4	C-4	C-4	C-4	C-4	C-4	C-4	AT
	F/O	W/U	W/U	RHA	RHA	OK	OK	O	O	O	O	O	O	O	O	RSY	RSY	O	RHA	RHA	O	FDS
COBOURG — Midland — May 11/44								NC	NC	NC	NC	C-6	C-6	C-6	C-6	C-6	C-6	C-6	C-6	C-6	C-6	C-6
								F/O	F/O	WUB	O	O	O	O	O	O	O	O	O	O	O	RHA
FERGUS — Collingwood — Nov.18/44														NC	NC	NC	C-9	C-9	C-9	C-9	C-9	AT
													F/O	RHA	WUB	O	O	O	O	O	FDS
FRONTENAC — Kingston — Oct.26/43	NC	NC	NC	NC	9-L	9-L	9-L	C-1	C-1	C-1	C-1	C-1	C-1	C-1	C-1	C-1	C-1	C-1	C-1	HX	HX	AT
	F/O	O/P	RHA	W/U	OSC	OK	OK	O	O	O	O	O	O	O	O	RLI	RLI	RHA	RHA	WUB	O	FDH
GUELPH — Collingwood — May 9/44								NC	NC	NC	C-8	C-8	C-8	C-8	C-8	C-8	C-8	C-8	C-8	C-8	C-8	AT
								F/O	F/O	WUB	O	O	O	O	O	O	O	O	O	O	O	FDQ
HAWKESBURY — Quebec City — June 14/44									NC	NC	NC	AT	C-7	C-7	C-7	C-7	C-7	C-7	C-7	C-7	AT	AT
									O/P	F/O	WUB	O	O	O	O	O	O	O	O	O	O	FDS
LINDSAY — Midland — Nov.15/43		NC	NC	NC	NC	AT	W-5	WD	WG	WG	WG	41H	41H	41H	41H	41H	41M	AT	AT	AT	AT	FDS
		F/O	O/P	F/O	WUB	O	RHA	OK	OK	OK	OK	OK	OK	OK	OK	OK	OK	RDV	RSB	RSB	RSB	FDS
LOUISBURG — Quebec City — Dec.13/43			NC	NC	NC	NC	WD	WG	WG	WG	41H	41H	41H	41H	41M	AT	AT	AT	AT	RSB	RSB	RSB
			F/O	RHA	RHA	WUB	O/P	OK	OK	OK	OK	OK	OK	OK	O/P	O	O	O	O/P	RSB	RSB	RSB
NORSYD — Quebec City — Dec.22/43			NC	NC	NC	NC	NC	W-7	W-7	W-7	W-7	W-7	W-7	W-7	C-2	C-2	C-2	C-2	C-2	C-2	AT	AT
			F/O	RIN	RIN	RIN	WUB	O	O	O	O	O	O	O	O	O	O	O	O	O	RHA	RHA
NORTH BAY — Collingwood — Oct.25/43	NC	NC	NC	NC	9-L	9-L	9-L	C-4	C-4	C-4	C-4	C-4	C-4	C-4	C-4	C-4	C-4	C-4	C-2	C-2	C-3	AT
	F/O	O/P	W/U	RHA	OSC	OK	OK	O	O	O	O	O	O	O	RSY	RSY	O	WUB	O	O	O	FDS
OWEN SOUND — Collingwood — Nov.17/43		NC	NC	NC	9-L	9-L	9-L	C-2	C-2	C-2	C-2	C-2	C-7	C-7	C-7	C-7	C-7	C-7	C-7	AT	AT	AT
		F/O	O/P	W/U	OSC	OK	OK	O	O	O	O	O	O	O	O	RHA	RHA	RHA	WUB	O	O	FDS
RIVIERE du LOUP — Quebec City — Nov.21/43		NC	NC	NC	NC	NC	NC	W-3	W-3	W-3	W-3	W-3	W-3	C-3	C-3	C-3	C-3	C-3	C-3	C-3	AT	AT
		F/O	O/P	RHA	WUB	RHA	RHA	RHA	RHA	RHA	O	O	O	O	RBE	RBE	O	N/O	O	O	O	FDS
ST. LAMBERT — Quebec City — May 27/44								NC	NC	NC	NC	C-6	C-6	C-6	C-6	C-6	C-6	C-6	C-6	C-6	C-6	AT
								F/O	F/O	RDA	WUB	O	O	O	RBE	O	O	O	O	RLN	O	FDJ
TRENTONIAN — Kingston — Dec.1/43			NC	NC	NC	NC	NC	WD	WG	WG	WG	41H	41H	41H	41H	41H	41H					
			O/P	F/O	WUB	O	RHA	OK	OK	OK	OK	OK	OK	OK	OK	OK	OK					
WHITBY — Midland — June 6/44									NC	NC	NC	NC	C-4	C-4	C-4	C-4	C-4	C-4	C-4	C-4	C-4	AT
									F/O	F/O	RSH	WUB	O	O	O	O	O	O	O	O	O	FDS

Revised Flower Class (I.E.), ex RN

Year columns: first 2 months = 1943 (Nov–Dec); next 12 = 1944 (Jan–Dec); last 7 = 1945 (Jan–Jul). Each ship has two data lines.

NAME of SHIP / Built at / Commissioned	Nov	Dec	Jan	Feb	Mar	Apr	May	Jun	Jul	Aug	Sep	Oct	Nov	Dec	Jan	Feb	Mar	Apr	May	Jun	Jul
FOREST HILL — Port Glasgow — Dec.1/43		NC	NC	C-3	C-3	C-3	C-3	C-3	C-3	C-3	C-3	C-3	C-3	C-3	C-3	C-3	C-3	C-3	HX	HX	AT
		FOK	WUK	O	O	O	O	O	O	O	O	O	O	O	RLI	RLI	RLI	WUB	O	O	FDS
GIFFARD — Aberdeen — Nov.10/43	NC	C-1	C-1	C-1	C-1	C-1	C-1	C-1	C-1	C-1	C-1	C-1	C-1	C-1	C-1	C-1	C-1	C-1	C-1	AT	AT
	FOK	WUK	O	O	O	O	O	O	O	O	O	O	O	O	RLI	RLI	WUB	O	O	AT	FDS
LONG BRANCH — Glasgow — Jan.5/44			NC	NC	WG	C-5	C-5	C-5	C-5	C-5	C-5	C-5	C-5	C-5	C-5	C-5	HX	HX			
			FOK	WUK	O	O	RSN	O	O	O	O	O	O	O	O	O	O	FDH			
MIMICO — Sunderland — Feb.8/44				NC	NC	NC	WG	WG	WG	WG	PO	NO	NO	NO	NO	NO	NO	NO	NO	AT	AT
				FOK	WUK	WUK	OK	OK	OK	OK	OK	OK	OK	OK	OK	OK	RCM	RCM	OK	O/P	FDS

	1944 Jan.	Feb.	Mar.	Apr.	May	June	July	Aug.	Sep.	Oct.	Nov.	Dec.	1945 Jan.	Feb.	Mar.	Apr.	May	June	July	Aug.	Sep.
	NF/W/U	NF/0	C-1/0	C-1/0	WG/OK	WG/OK	WG/OK	WG/OK													
	W-6/0	W-6/0	W-6/0	W-6/0	W-2/0	W-2/0	W-2/RLI	W-2/RLI	W-2/RLI	W-2/RLI	W-2/WUB	W-2/0	W-2/0	W-2/0	W-2/0	W-2/0	W-2/0	AT/FDS			
	PE/0	PE/0	PE/O/P	W-4/0	W-3/0	W-1/0	QF/0	QF/0	QF/RCA	W-1/RCA	W-1/0	W-1/WUB	W-1/0	W-1/0	W-1/0	W-1/0	W-1/0	AT/FDQ			
	W-2/0	W-2/RLI	W-2/RLI	W-2/RLI	AT/RHA	AT/WUB	C-4/0	C-4/0	WD/OK	41H/OK	41H/OK	41H/OK	41H/OK	41H/OK	41H/OK	41M/OK	41H/OK	AT/0	AT/FDS		
	C-4/0	C-4/0	C-4/0	WG/OK	WG/OK	WG/OK	WG/OK	WG/OK	AT/RLI	AT/O/P	PA/0	PA/0	PE/RES	PE/RES	PE/RES	PE/0	PE/0	PA/0	PA/0	PA/0	

Revised Flower Class (I.E.), 1943-1944 Programme

NAME of SHIP / Built at / Commissioned	1944 May	June	July	Aug.	Sep.	Oct.	Nov.	Dec.	1945 Jan.	Feb.	Mar.	Apr.	May	June	July
ASBESTOS / Quebec City / June 16/44	NC/F/O	NC/F/O	C-2/WUB	C-2/0	C-2/0	C-2/0	C-2/0	C-2/0	C-2/0	C-2/0	C-2/0	C-2/0	C-2/0	AT	AT/FDS
BEAUHARNOIS / Quebec City / Sept.25/44				NC/F/O	NC/F/O	NC/WUB	C-3/0	C-4/0	C-4/0	C-4/0	C-4/0	C-4/0	C-4/0	AT	AT/FDS
BELLEVILLE / Kingston / Oct.19/44						NC/F/O	NC/RHA	NC/RHA	NC/RHA	NC/WUB	C-5/0	C-5/0	C-5/0	AT	AT/FDS
LACHUTE / Quebec City / Oct.26/44					NC/F/O	NC/F/O	NC/WUB	C-5/0	C-5/0	C-5/0	C-5/0	C-5/0	C-5/0	AT	AT/FDS
MERRITTONIA / Quebec City / Nov.10/44							NC/F/O	NC/F/O	NC/WUB	C-7/0	C-7/0	C-7/0	C-7/0	AT	AT/FDS
PARRY SOUND / Midland / Aug.30/44			NC/F/O	NC/F/O	NC/WUB	C-7/0	C-7/0	C-7/0	C-7/0	C-7/N/O	C-7/0	C-7/0		AT	AT/FDS
PETERBOROUGH / Kingston / June 1/44	NC/F/O	NC/WUB	NC/0	C-6/0	C-6/0	C-6/0	C-6/0	C-6/0	C-6/0	C-6/0	C-6/0	C-6/RLN	C-6/0	AT	AT/FDS
SMITHS FALLS / Kingston / Nov.28/44							NC/F/O	NC/F/O	NC/F/O	NC/RHA	C-2/WUB	C-2/0	AT/0	AT	AT/FDS
STELLARTON / Quebec City / Sept.29/44					NC/F/O	NC/F/O	NC/WUB	C-3/RSN	C-3/0	C-3/0	C-3/0	C-3/0	C-3/0	AT	AT/FDS
STRATHROY / Midland / Nov.20/44							NC/F/O	NC/F/O	NC/RSB	NC/RSB	HX/WUB	HX/0	HX/0	HX/0	AT/FDS
THORLOCK / Midland / Nov.13/44							NC/F/O	NC/F/O	NC/WUB	C-9/0	C-9/0	C-9/0	C-9/0	AT	AT/FDS
WEST YORK / Midland / Oct.6/44					NC/F/O	NC/F/O	NC/RHA	NC/WUB	C-5/0	C-5/0	C-5/0	C-5/0	C-5/0	AT	AT/FDS

Castle Class, ex-RN

NAME of SHIP / Built at / Commissioned	1943 Nov.	Dec.	1944 Jan.	Feb.	Mar.	Apr.	May	June	July	Aug.	Sep.	Oct.	Nov.	Dec.	1945 Jan.	Feb.	Mar.	Apr.	May	June	July	Aug.	Sep.
ARNPRIOR / Belfast / June 8/44							NC/FOK	NC/WUK	C-1/0	C-1/0	C-1/0	C-1/0	C-1/0	C-1/0	C-1/0	C-1/0	C-1/0	C-1/0	C-1/0	AT/RSN	AT/RSN	AT	AT/FDH
BOWMANVILLE / Sunderland / Sept.28/44										NC/FOK	NC/WUK	C-4/0	C-4/0	C-4/0	C-4/0	C-4/0	C-4/0	C-4/0	AT/0	AT/0	AT/0	AT/0	TR
COPPER CLIFF / Blyth / July 25/44								NC/FOK	NC/FOK	C-6/WUK	C-7/0	C-7/0	C-7/0	C-7/0	C-7/0	C-7/0	C-7/0	C-7/0	AT/O/P	PA/O/P	PA/0	PA	PA/FDE
HESPELER / Leith / Feb.28/44		NC/FOK	NC/FOK	NC/WUK	C-5/0	C-5/0	C-5/0	C-5/0	C-5/0	C-5/0	C-5/0	C-5/0	C-5/0	C-5/0	C-8/RHA	C-9/RHA	C-8/N/O	C-8/RLI	C-8/O/P	AT	PA/FDE		
HUMBERSTONE / Glasgow / Sept.6/44										NC/FOK	NC/WUK	C-8/0	C-8/0	C-8/0	C-8/0	C-8/0	C-8/0	C-8/0	AT/0	PA/O/P	PA/O/P	PA	PA/FDE
HUNTSVILLE / Troon / June 6/44							NC/FOK	NC/WUK	C-5/0	C-5/0	C-5/0	C-5/0	C-5/0	C-5/0	C-5/0	C-5/0	C-5/0	C-5/0	AT/0	AT/RHA	AT/RHA	AT/RHA	IHA
KINCARDINE / South Bank / June 19/44							NC/FOK	NC/WUK	C-2/0	C-2/0	C-2/0	C-2/0	C-2/0	C-2/0	C-2/0	C-2/0	C-2/0	C-2/0	C-2/0	AT/0	AT/0	AT/0	AT/FDH
LEASIDE / South Bank / Aug.21/44									NC/FOK	NC/WUK	C-8/0	C-8/0	C-8/0	C-8/0	C-8/0	C-8/0	C-8/0	AT/0	PA/O/P	PA/O/P	PA/0	PA	PA/FDE
ORANGEVILLE / Leith / Apr.24/44					NC/FOK	NC/WUK	C-1/0	C-1/0	C-1/0	C-1/0	C-1/0	C-1/0	C-1/0	C-1/0	C-1/0	C-1/0	C-1/0	C-1/0	AT/RLI	AT/RLI	AT/RLI	AT	AT/FDH
PETROLIA / Belfast / June 29/44							NC/FOK	NC/WUK	C-4/0	C-4/0	C-4/0	C-4/0	C-4/0	C-4/0	C-4/0	C-4/0	C-4/0	C-4/0	C-4/0	AT/0	AT/0	AT/0	AT/RCA
ST. THOMAS / South Bank / May 4/44					NC/FOK	NC/WUK	WD/OK	C-3/0	C-3/0	C-3/0	C-3/0	C-3/0	C-3/0	C-3/0	C-3/0	C-3/0	C-3/0	C-3/0	AT/0	AT/RHA	AT/RHA	AT/O/P	FDE
TILLSONBURG / Port Glasgow / June 29/44							NC/FOK	NC/FOK	NC/WUK	C-6/0	C-6/0	C-6/0	C-6/0	C-6/0	C-6/0	C-6/0	C-6/0	C-6/RLN	C-6/0	AT/0	AT/0	AT/0	AT/FDH

INDEX

Figures in bold refer to photographs in Part I

PHOTOCREDITS

It is fitting that one-third of the photographs which illustrate this book should have come from individuals who served Canada at sea a half-century ago. Their names are listed below against the numbers of the pages where those photographs appear. We are grateful also to the institutions whose photographs enrich our book, in particular the National Archives of Canada, whose photographs are identified by their negative numbers, the British Ministry of Defence (MoD), and the Marine Museum of the Great Lakes at Kingston, Ontario (MMGL).

PART I
Chapter One
Page 12:MMGL; 12:MMGL; 12:MMGL; 12:MMGL; 14:MMGL; 14:MMGL; 15:0.71.; 16:Milner Coll.; 20:Port Arthur Shipbuilding Co. Ltd.; 20:E.2095; 21:PA-136247; 22:H.762.
Chapter Two
Page 25:CH.2346A; 25:PMR 92-104; 26:Milner Coll.; 27:PA-184189; 27:0.14-13; 29:J. Hughes; 29:NF.338; 31 :PA-116838; 31:PA-184186; 32:0.1678; 33:0.326-1; 33:MMGL; 37:MMGL.
Chapter Three
Page 39:0.1869.; 40:P. George; 43:Sam Langford; 43:PMR 92-102; 46:NP.1040.; 46:Macpherson Coll.; 47: CN.3836; 47:J. Tice; 48:J. Tice; 48:PMR.92-105; 49:MoD; 50:0.3791.
Chapter Four
Page 53:PMR.83-397; 54:J. Tice; 55:PMR.92-103; 56:PMR.92-100; 58:PA-184193; 59:PA-184125; 62:PA-139916; 63:PA-112918; 64:PA-184200; 64:PA-184194; 65:USN.
Chapter Five
Page 67:0.14-10; 67:PA-113916; 68:F. McLachlan; 69:MMGL; 71:PA-184191; 72:PA-184196; 76:JT.440; 76:Z.1575; 77:PA-184199; 79:PA-116299; 81:PA-184198; 81:Z.1426.
Chapter Six
Page 83:PA-184192; 85:HS.1355-21; 85:Macpherson Coll.; 86:Macpherson Coll.; 87:Macpherson Coll.

PART II
1939-1940 Canadian Program, Pages 89-116

Agassiz:Macpherson Collection; *Alberni*:RCAF; *Algoma*:Macpherson Coll.; *Amherst*:Macpherson Coll.; *Arvida*:NAC HS.0555-2; *Baddeck*:A.824; *Barrie*:H.6672; *Battleford*:A. Cameron; *Brandon*:MoD; *Buctouche*:D. Trimingham; *Camrose*:F.Bamford; *Chambly*:K.423; *Chicoutimi*:E.2677; *Chilliwack*:H.2644; *Cobalt*:Macpherson Coll.; *Collingwood*:D. Piers; *Dauphin*:CN.2334; *Dawson*:RCAF; *Drumheller*:J. Hughes; *Dunvegan*:F. Keegan; *Edmundston*:R. Simon; *Galt*: CN.6137; *Kamloops*:N. Dickinson; *Kamsack*:R. Jackson; *Kenogami*:A. Cameron; *Lethbridge*:SY.54-23; *Lévis*:0.326-1; *Louisburg*:MoD; *Lunenburg*:CN.3833; *Matapedia*:W. Ormsby; *Moncton*:GM.1161; *Moose Jaw*:C. Lancaster; *Morden*:National Maritime Museum; *Nanaimo*:F.4544; *Napanee*:CN.3805; *Oakville*:Shiels; *Orillia*:J. Tice; *Pictou*:J. Pegg; *Prescott*:G. Kirtley; *Quesnel*:USN; *Rimouski*:WRN.1204; *Rosthern*:J. Hughes; *Sackville*:C.Love; *Saskatoon*:RCAF; *Shawinigan*:D.LeRoy; *Shediac*:RCAF; *Sherbrooke*:GM.0331; *Sorel*:W. Derrett; *Sudbury*:F.3365; *Summerside*:P. McEntyre; *The Pas*:Macpherson Coll.; *Trail*:NF.93; *Wetaskiwin*:G. Woods; *Weyburn*:J. Britten.

1939-1940 Program, Built for the RN, Pages 117-122

Arrowhead:NP.1009; *Bittersweet*:R.243; *Eyebright*:J. Tice; *Fennel*:Macpherson Coll.; *Hepatica*:CN.3468; *Mayflower*:A. Forsythe; *Snowberry*:MoD; *Spikenard*:NP.348; *Trillium*:US Coastguard; *Windflower*:Macpherson Coll.

1940-1941 Short-Forecastle Program, Pages 123-126

Brantford:R.M. Smillie; *Dundas*:E.2681; *Midland*:HS.0343-110; *New Westminster*:E.2097; *Timmins*:D. LeRoy; *Vancouver*:R. Parker.

1940-1941 Revised Program, Pages 127-132

Calgary:S.424; *Charlottetown*:CN.3636; *Fredericton*:GM.1149; *Halifax*:G. Johnson; *Kitchener*:SM.1108; *La Malbaie*:R.128; *Port Arthur*:CN.3564; *Regina*:NP.843; *Ville de Québec*:J. Allan; *Woodstock*:Macpherson Coll.

1942-1943 Increased Endurance Program, Pages 133-141

Atholl:CN.3597; *Cobourg*:M.879; *Fergus*:D. Trimingham; *Frontenac*:K.506; *Guelph*:MMGL; *Hawkesbury*:QS.0002-2; *Lindsay*:G. Thomson; *Norsyd*:D. Willcock; *North Bay*:W. McMullen; *Owen Sound*:P. Hardy; *Rivière du Loup*:L.5887; *St. Lambert*:G. Woods; *Trentonian*:D. Trimingham; *Whitby*:Watson's Studio.

1943-1944 Increased Endurance Program, Pages 142-148

Asbestos:W. Milroy; *Beauharnois*:QS.0011-4; *Belleville*:A.1023; *Lachute*:Z.1198; *Merrittonia*:Shiels; *Parry Sound*:J. W. Bald; *Peterborough*:Macpherson Coll.; *Smiths Falls*:S.3210; *Stellarton*:J. Picton; *Strathroy*:0.15164; *Thorlock*:D. Trimingham; *West York*:Z.1200.

British-Built Increased Endurance Corvettes, Pages 149-151

Forest Hill:J. Hall, Gourock; *Giffard*:P. Robinson; *Long Branch*:J. Hume; *Mimico*:MoD.

Castle Class Corvettes, British-Built, Pages 152-158

Arnprior:MoD; *Bowmanville*:MoD; *Copper Cliff*:MoD; *Hespeler*:A.389; *Humberstone*:R. Simon; *Huntsville*:R.1945; *Kincardine*:MoD; *Leaside*:W. H. Parry; *Orangeville*:Henry Robb Ltd.; *Petrolia*:MoD; *St. Thomas*:J. McEntee; *Tillsonburg*:MoD.

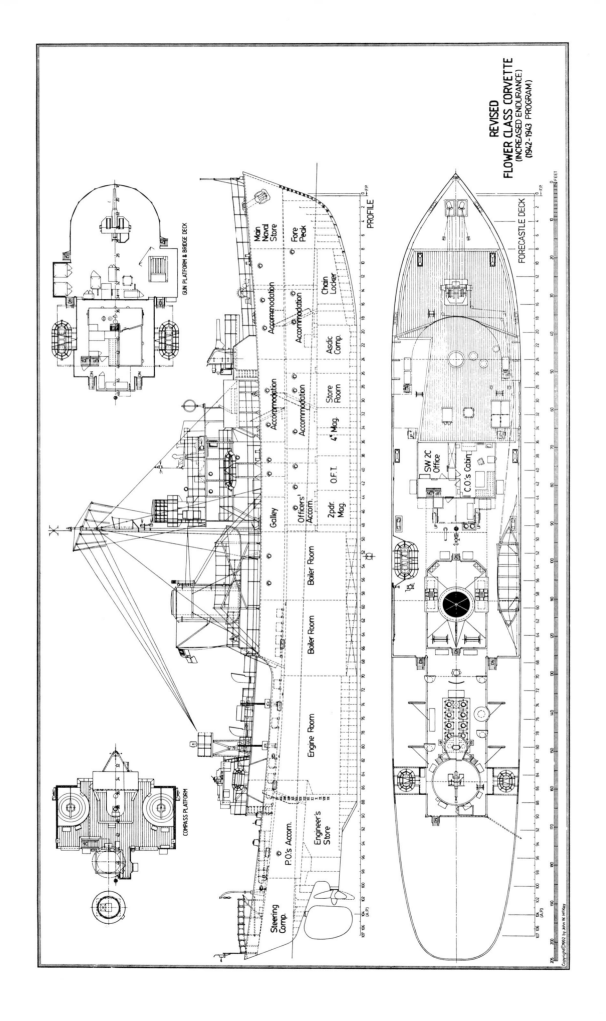

REVISED
FLOWER CLASS CORVETTE
(INCREASED ENDURANCE)
(1942-1943 PROGRAM)

GUN PLATFORM & BRIDGE DECK

COMPASS PLATFORM

PROFILE

Main Naval Store
Fore Peak
Accommodation
Accommodation
Chain Locker
Asdic Comp.
Accommodation
Accommodation
Store Room
4" Mag.
Galley
Officers' Accom.
2pdr. Mag.
O.F.T.
Boiler Room
Boiler Room
Boiler Room
Engine Room
P.O.'s Accom.
Engineer's Store
Steering Comp.

FORECASTLE DECK

SW 2C Office
C.O.'s Cabin

FP
FP

FEET

Copyright ©1993 by John W. McKay

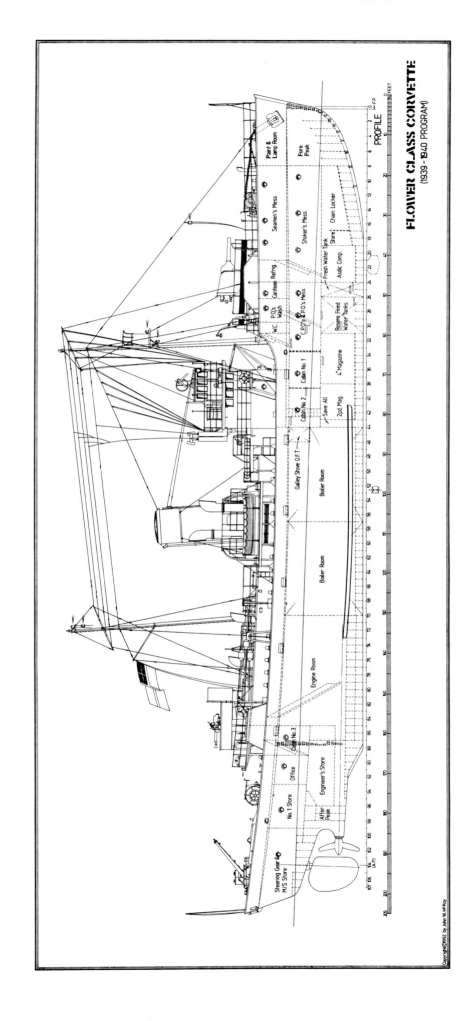

FLOWER CLASS CORVETTE

(1939 - 1940 PROGRAM)

PROFILE

Paint & Lamp Room

Fore Peak

Seamen's Mess

Stoker's Mess

Fresh Water Tank

Chain Locker

Canteen Refrig

Asdic Comp.

W.C. P.O.s Wash

P.O's & P.O's Mess

Reserve Feed Water Tanks

Cabin No 1

4" Magazine

Cabin No 2

Save All

2pd Mag

Galley Stove O.F.T.

Boiler Room

Boiler Room

Engine Room

Cabin No 3

Office

Engineer's Store

After Peak

No 1 Store

Steering Gear
M/S Store

Copyright ©1992 by John W. McKay

FEET

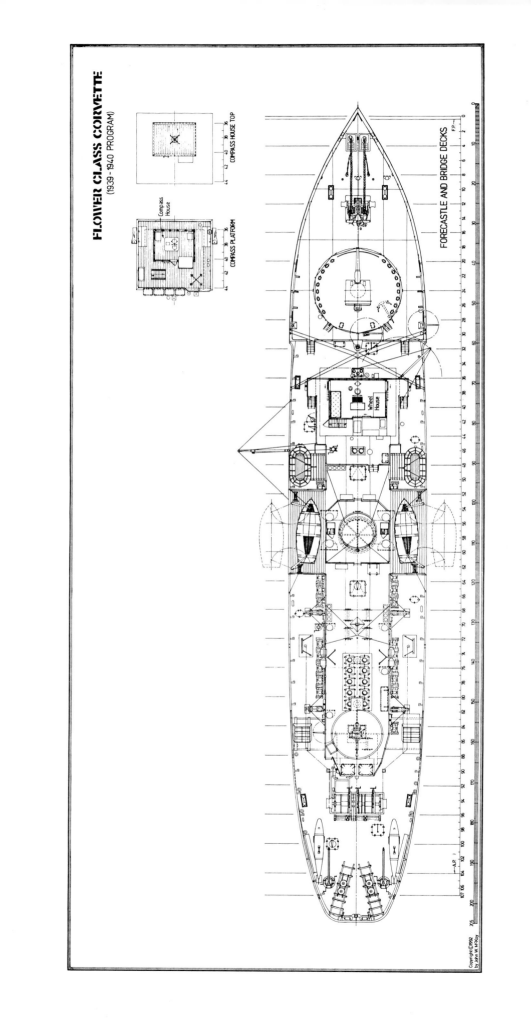

FLOWER CLASS CORVETTE

(1939 - 1940 PROGRAM)

COMPASS HOUSE TOP

Compass House

COMPASS PLATFORM

FORECASTLE AND BRIDGE DECKS

Wheel House